Equity-Oriented
Critical Curricula

Equity-Oriented Critical Curricula

Envisioning Hope with Students

Angela Miller-Hargis
Delane A. Bender-Slack

ROWMAN & LITTLEFIELD
Lanham • Boulder • New York • London

Published by Rowman & Littlefield
An imprint of The Rowman & Littlefield Publishing Group, Inc.
4501 Forbes Boulevard, Suite 200, Lanham, Maryland 20706
www.rowman.com

86-90 Paul Street, London EC2A 4NE, United Kingdom

British Library Cataloguing in Publication Information Available

Library of Congress Cataloging-in-Publication Data

Names: Miller-Hargis, Angela, 1965– author. | Bender-Slack, Delane A., author.
Title: Equity-oriented critical curricula : envisioning hope with students / Angela Miller-Hargis and Delane A. Bender-Slack.
Description: Lanham, Maryland : Rowman & Littlefield, 2023. | Includes bibliographical references and index. | Summary: "Designed to balance theory and praxis, this book offers opportunities for teachers to begin building integrated critical literacy curricula that prioritizes the lived experiences and insights of their students"— Provided by publisher.
Identifiers: LCCN 2022050910 (print) | LCCN 2022050911 (ebook) | ISBN 9781475866933 (cloth) | ISBN 9781475866940 (paperback) | ISBN 9781475866957 (epub)
Subjects: LCSH: Critical pedagogy. | Critical thinking—Study and teaching. | Language arts—Curricula. | Educational equalization.
Classification: LCC LC196 .M55 2023 (print) | LCC LC196 (ebook) | DDC 370.11/5—dc23/eng/20221228
LC record available at https://lccn.loc.gov/2022050910
LC ebook record available at https://lccn.loc.gov/2022050911

*To my grandchildren—Everly Sullivan, Amora
Rosemarie, and Lennox Finley—
My hope is that you may always be surrounded by teachers who value your
potential by seeing everything that makes you unique and wonderful.
—Angela*

*To my siblings—Darby, Jeff, Eric, and Jason—
All we learned, all we accomplished, and all we hoped for,
I am beyond blessed to have shared with you along the way.
—Laney*

Contents

Foreword ix

Acknowledgments xiii

Introduction xv

Chapter 1: The Intersection of Critical Literacy and Curricular
Conversations: Conceiving of Social Justice 1

Chapter 2: Critical Conversations Curriculum Charts: Intersection
of Curriculum as Conversation and Critical Literacy as
Transformative Space 17

Chapter 3: Developing Critical Literacy Lessons through
Meaningful Themes: Planning for Emerging Opportunities 31

Chapter 4: Interdisciplinary Critical Literacies: Incorporating
Critical Literacy Lessons in the Disciplines Using Texts That
Matter 43

Chapter 5: International Classrooms: Global Networks and Leading
with Hope 61

Chapter 6: Obstacles to Critical Literacy Planning: Shifting from
Unit to Lesson Planning 75

Chapter 7: Equity-Based Educational Planning: Moving toward
Justice and Shared Power 87

References 95

Index 99

Foreword

Information is a ubiquitous and ever-growing aspect of contemporary life, and each of us is assaulted daily with all types of messaging through our online presence, our use of media sources such as streaming and cable services, and through our consumption of print through magazines, books, and newspapers. Billboards still compete for our attention along the highway, and bumper stickers and license plates still compel us to consider their significance. In essence, as humans we communicate in such multiple and varied ways, we often don't think deeply about the messages or the meanings we encounter or project as we interact with the world. What we wear, what we say, or what we don't say all create space for meaning making, and young people are intimately involved in these ways of knowing and being as they go about their lives. Unfortunately, they are not often explicitly taught about or asked to reflect upon how they impact or are impacted by the information—the knowledge streams—of their lives.

So much of what we learn—and the biases and stereotypes we embrace—are acquired with little reflection. We learn so much at the dinner table without conscious thought or deep consideration. We assume that what we know is the norm, the way things are, the ways things have always been. And yet, with social undertakings such as #BlackLivesMatter, #MeToo, and #TimesUp as well as other reform and revolutionary movements across the world, we come to realize that our ideas of the way things are and always have been need rethinking and deeper—more critical—thought.

Yet even with tools to help us understand the world and remain in constant contact through social messaging, many of us become overwhelmed by those encounters. The constant barrage of notices often creates the need to retreat from the very world we are living in and connecting to through the devices we hold in our hands. Others of us attempt to engage, but often the complexity of negotiating the modern world becomes a dive down a rabbit hole that keeps us off balance and questioning if we know anything at all. Determining how to navigate the world of knowing and knowledge, as well as input and action, needs to be addressed as a way of reckoning with issues of encounter and power and an increasingly smaller world that affects us all.

Given the complexity of our shared spaces as citizens of particular communities and nations as well as inhabitants of the world, we need to develop ways of interpreting and responding to situations and circumstances that we encounter. In essence, we need to ask questions that attend to our engagement with the world in ways that can move us from being overwhelmed to ways of thoughtful actions that are beneficial for ourselves and others. We need to discover ways to determine what is equitable and kind as we encounter conflicting messages that at best can confuse us and at worst are duplicitous and dangerous ideologies that prescribe actions harmful to others' well-being and safety. How do we learn to "read" the messaging we encounter in our lives so we might be more responsive and less reactive? How do we decipher the evidence given us? The misinformation? And how do we get to the place of recognizing the complexity of life and knowledge in our social worlds? And most importantly, how do we engage in habits of thought that will discipline our minds to be more critically aware, hopeful, and thoughtful as we address what we encounter through print and imagery?

In this text, Angela Miller-Hargis and Delane Bender-Slack take on these questions and issues while recognizing the power teachers have in guiding students toward a more just and equitable world. Engaged in thoughtful ways of working through pedagogical circumstances that allow teachers to work toward hope and equity, Miller-Hargis and Bender-Slack balance theory and practice so teachers might begin building students' literacies that encourage students to connect their knowledge, their lived experiences, and their insights to a curriculum that provides possibilities of equity and hope, empowerment, and critical knowing of how language and texts impact their lives.

In addition, they forefront the reality that literacies are never politically neutral, but are enmeshed in often multiple and conflicting networks of social, political, cultural, and historical contexts. In this volume, they have worked to encourage teachers to develop curricular engagements that invite students into ongoing conversations that address social circumstances with tenets of critical literacies to produce spaces of possibilities that can have a direct effect on students' lives. Utilizing Applebee's (1996) conception of curriculum for its pedagogical possibilities, Miller-Hargis and Bender-Slack first address five curricular structures organized along a continuum based on the extent that encourages or discourages the expansion of disciplinary conversations. They note these structures as catalog, collection, sequential, episodic, and integrated curricula. Embracing a more integrated curriculum structure, these authors encourage a curriculum that is conceived as "domains for culturally significant conversations" that provide ways of regarding curriculum as more than just what is learned, but how it is learned as well (Applebee,

1996). In ways that link with critical literacies, an integrated curriculum resists a structure of knowledge being disseminated in a top-down approach, but is rather constructed within the spaces by those involved in dialogue.

Moving beyond disciplinary conversations, however, Miller-Hargis and Bender-Slack encourage teachers to create spaces for students to empower themselves through critical literacy practices that reflect equity and hope. Through curricular instances that connect to aspects similar to those of Langer's (1995; 2015) concept of envisionments from literature and disciplinary knowledge, students' embrace the possibilities of an equitable world through engagements about and from disciplinary texts that include conversations that question aspects of power as well as disenfranchisement with the potential to disrupt the status quo both within the classroom and beyond it. As they note in their introduction, such a curriculum creates spaces for students to explore, investigate, and consider all manner of interpretive possibility.

Ultimately, this text invites teachers to reside within a curricular space of possibility that includes students, students' hopes, and student voices. Residence within a space of inclusion that honors all voices while also disrupting the status quo, however, can often produce its own multiplex of rabbit holes. Yet Miller-Hargis and Bender-Slack gently build and guide readers through practices that allow teachers and students to collaborate and strive toward common goals that embrace all learners in ways that allow for both individual and classroom agency and knowing as well as critically questioning and problem-posing. It is through this work that teachers and students come to recognize the dignity and possibility of their own lives and work while allowing for ways to negotiate the world and the conflicting messages that inundate us in the complex world in which we live.

—Holly Johnson

Acknowledgments

We wish to acknowledge, first and foremost, our brilliant doctoral advisor, Dr. Robert Burroughs. While the first few months of graduate school were challenging (to say the least), your steadfast guidance allowed us to push forward. Your research on curricular conversations and disciplinary discourse became foundational in our own understanding of what transformative classrooms might be, and your powerful pedagogy within the context of our doctoral courses became a model for our own instruction as teacher educators. We will always appreciate your availability both in and out of the classroom, a gift you continue to extend. Your enthusiasm for our work both humbles and motivates us. As such, we recognize your contribution to our continued development as hopeful teacher educators and educational researchers. Thank you, Bob, for all you are and all you do!

We also would like to thank the teacher candidates with whom we work, especially those who so generously contributed to this book (Emma Bruggeman, Katherine Kinney, Michelle Kohler, Olivia Masuck-Lane, Morgan (Clinton) Schutte, Ericka Vickers, and "Isabel") who allowed us to utilize their critical literacy lesson plans and Critical Conversations Curriculum Charts for inclusion in this book. Engaging with, learning from, and interacting with each and every one of our teacher candidates individually and collectively are at the heart of what inspires us to improve ourselves and our teaching practices. The classroom experiences we have shared with you are the impetus for the writing of this text and generated the energy that sustained its completion.

Thank you to our justice-oriented colleagues here and around the globe who continue to inspire, question, challenge, and support us in this important endeavor. It is good to know that we are not alone in envisioning and working toward a better future. Your passion and hope fuels us!

I, Laney, would like to give a shout out to my ride-or-die family and friends, who wish for and aspire to equity and justice, but especially much gratitude to my parents (Robert and Mary Bender) who showed me that serving others through our professions is the noblest and most necessary work of all.

I, Angela, would like to acknowledge my family, especially my husband, Matt; my children, Anamarie, Alex, and Livvy; my mother, Marie; my father, Larry, who is no longer with us; and my sister, Andrea DeMiceli. All of you have taught me that engaging in deep and meaningful exchanges of ideas is critical to every aspect of our personal and professional growth. You are my home, my joy, my everything.

Introduction

This book has been a long time in the making. While it's easy to point to the period of time where we came together as doctoral students, the truth is that our understanding of the necessity of such a book started decades before we met in graduate school or began to study the work of researchers and theorists and educational policy makers.

ANGELA'S STORY

In December 1986, I was a newly minted elementary educator facing an interviewing firing squad of four individuals, attempting to prove my suitability for teaching in an inner-city parochial school. I was not quite twenty-two years old and, having graduated a semester early from a Jesuit university near the elementary school, I was contacted by the school principal to interview for a full-day kindergarten teaching position. I was elated! The teacher I was replacing had some type of medical issue and would not be returning after the Christmas break, so I dutifully reported to the cafeteria on New Year's Eve to face the principal, the pastor, the president of the Parent-Teacher Organization, and one of the teachers who had volunteered for the search committee. Other than the PTO president, the faces of the interviewers looked exactly like my own.

I was a young, lower middle-class, White woman, armed with a traditional liberal arts education, complete with a hefty dose of theology and philosophy and a state teaching license with ink barely dry. I felt confident that I could answer their questions with ease, and I knew that I would do amazing things if I got this job. I can honestly say I remember very few of the queries made during that two-hour interrogation, except for one: "What skills or understanding do you bring to this job that will allow you to work with the children at this school? You realize, of course, our school is 99.7 percent Black and a majority of our families operate below the poverty line."

I had, in fact, *not* realized that. Except for the commute to and from the university, I rarely ventured out of my own neighborhood and surrounding areas, yet I didn't even hesitate. I stated, "I don't think that matters, really. Regardless of what color children are, black, white, or orange with purple polka dots, children are children, and I am sure that I will be effective in the classroom." Looking back now, my response is cringeworthy, really, and I shudder every time I think of my certain, even arrogant, response.

Truth is, I got that job, and I started teaching the first of the year. It didn't take me more than a week to realize how completely wrong I had been and how ineffectual a teacher with little to no knowledge of her students' backgrounds, families, and culture could be. The school had no hot lunch program and, although students were expected to brown bag their lunch daily, many of my kindergartners would come without food regularly. It was not uncommon for my students to arrive without socks or close-toed shoes, and once I even discovered one of my students had no undergarments under her uniform skirt. The children all lived in the neighborhood and a majority walked to the school, and although they were not supposed to arrive on the grounds before 7:45, it was not uncommon to have a gathering of a dozen or more children near the entrance of the school as early as 7:15.

Luckily, I was surrounded by amazing colleagues who mentored me a great deal in that first year and beyond. I learned to keep snacks, peanut butter, and bread in my classroom at all times, and the school regularly purchased an assortment of shoes, socks, underwear, and even uniform items in a variety of sizes that were kept in a converted closet that was made to look like a store. While the children were expected to attend Catholic Mass and received religious instruction daily, we celebrated Kwanzaa in conjunction with Christmas activities, and I learned the songs and principles of my students' heritage. I began to volunteer at a local nonprofit that allowed teachers to "shop" for educational materials for free in return for volunteer hours, thus ensuring my students would not have to worry about school supplies at home.

I was blessed to have an amazing principal and pastor that shared their own experiences and helped guide me as both an educator and an individual. Over the three years I taught at the school, I learned how little I knew about people outside of my insular "bubble," and the deficit view of learning I had acquired through my own education and culture was challenged. It was the first time I truly began to understand that, as much as I wanted it to be, education may not be the great equalizer I was always taught it could be. There was so much more to learning than what was occurring in my classroom. And I began to question why I had been allowed to enter a teaching career with such a limited view of what it meant to be a culturally competent educator.

A seed was planted in those first few difficult and hectic years of teaching. Ultimately, this vignette is not about what I learned to do for my students but about what my students did for me. My students taught me far more than I ever taught them about life, learning, and mutual respect. While I moved on to other positions and continued to mature as a teacher, learner, and individual, no other job I ever had as an elementary educator affected me as profoundly. The cognitive dissonance I experienced in those initial teaching years remained dormant for many years and little did I realize the powerful roots it was growing.

LANEY'S STORY

I grew up in a lower middle-class, Catholic family, the fourth of five children. My mom was an elementary teacher and my dad a social worker. My grandparents, survivors of the Great Depression, and my parents, Baby Boomers, stressed the importance of an education as a way to financial success. Perhaps that is why my parents were disappointed when I decided to become a teacher. They knew that all-too-familiar road of tight budgets, cutting coupons, and supplemental summer jobs to try to make ends meet. There was never enough money, and it was always the source of arguments and stress.

My journey into education was happenstance, really. I loved my English classes, but when my mom found out I wanted to major in English, she said I couldn't afford to go to graduate school or graduate and not immediately have a job. So, I majored in English education instead. I loved reading and writing. And as time went on, I grew to love teaching. My first year of teaching, though, was a colossal struggle. At times I floundered. At times I forged ahead. At times I faked it. At times I fought. At times I failed. And at times, maybe for a few moments, I was fabulous.

In my first teaching position, I was on an interdisciplinary middle school team, teaching seventh and eighth graders in English Language Arts. The school was in a rural area that was just beginning to sell off farmland, one-story ranches, and trailer parks to real estate developers. It would, in the thirteen years I was there, become a rising, affluent suburb of strip malls, golf courses, and McMansions.

But when I started there, the middle school was housed in an old, fading brick building with no air conditioning, chipping paint, and leaky ceilings. It was, however, a fairly young and vibrant faculty, that would usher the community into the next phase of suburbanization. I grew, along with my students, as we engaged in writing workshops and read novels together. And the roots of my love for teaching were planted there. Those memories of teaching and learning are bittersweet.

There was one memorable boy named Jeremy. He was a seventh grader with curly red hair and freckles. Never outright defiant, he would just shrug when I asked to see his homework. A bit of a follower, he was happy to get into trouble when other boys in the class included him on the playground or in the hallways.

Since we followed the teaming model for middle schools, our faculty team met each day to address student issues. Jeremy's name frequently came up, and we realized he was not doing homework in all of his classes and was on the verge of failing seventh grade. We requested a conference with his parents, who came in one day in their jeans and concert t shirts sitting across from his team of teachers in button-downs and ties or dresses and jewelry.

We asked that Jeremy attend the conference as well and shared our concerns with his missing assignments and behavioral issues. After the list of complaints, and as I recall it, a rather lengthy list, Jeremy's dad had hit his frustration point. He suddenly turned to Jeremy, pointed at him, and sternly said, "That's it. No more cigarettes for you." The room was suddenly quiet, our eyes and mouths open wide. Nobody knew how to respond. My colleague, Mike, a veteran teacher who had grown up in the rural community, was the first to recover, and just said, "Well, I should hope not."

It was jarring, that cultural collision. To be honest, at the time, I did not see all of the power dynamics at play in that situation, but rather I perceived it as bad parenting. If only I had the tools and awareness to see it differently, to connect with his family, and to teach him differently.

Anyone who has spent any time in the field of education—time with students, parents, administrators, and other teachers—is aware of the plethora of justice issues. From standardized testing to the overidentification of students of color in special education, from top-down curriculum to institutionalized White supremacy, there is a lot to negotiate, resist, and confront. My work as a scholar, professor, and lifetime educator is meant to do just that.

OUR STORY OF CONVERGENCE

So, after thirteen years of Laney teaching in secondary ELA classrooms and eighteen years of Angela teaching ELA in elementary grades, our separate roads converged when we met in the doctoral program of an urban university, learning about curriculum from our shared mentor, and exploring critical literacy in our studies and then in our college classrooms. It was clear from the beginning that we shared similar personal and familial backgrounds, embraced a constructivist teaching philosophy, and anticipated a comparable career trajectory.

We will always be grateful to our remarkable academic advisor, Bob Burroughs, who first introduced us to the writings of *his* doctoral advisor and mentor, Arthur Applebee. He organized our first research project where we began to understand the significance of evaluating the levels of curricular conversations across disciplines, taking place before, during, and after teaching occurs. Together, we convinced Bob to allow us to develop an independent study that focused on defining social justice, and we committed to reading all we could on the social and political aspects of literacy learning and teaching, eventually leading to our commitment to critical literacy as both a theoretical foundation and a pedagogical practice.

Before long, an idea emerged: Was it possible to use the idea of conceiving of curriculum as "domains for culturally significant conversations" to improve the pedagogical practices of teachers? How could we emphasize to our own students, teacher candidates, and in-service educators alike, that literacy education is more than the dissemination of information, more than memorizing a list of facts and concepts, and far more than ensuring that their students know how to read and write in academic settings? Was it possible to ensure that the educators we taught could conceive of, design, and implement literacy lessons that are delivered to students in a critical and meaningful way? How could we do for our students that which was not done for us?

Once hired in academia, we both were teaching methods courses, building them from the ground up, so we decided we could merge curriculum and critical literacy into a hopeful and transformative method course. As we continued to struggle with our questions, we experimented with the use of various texts and in-class instructional processes at the various institutions where we taught. We conducted action research in our own post-secondary classrooms and presented at various conferences, seeking feedback on our failures and successes. We published articles that attempted to elucidate our current thinking about potential answers to our enquiries; we regularly revisited those same questions again and again, challenging our individual and collective understanding of what it means to empower teachers to build curricula with their students, colleagues, and communities. That work began fifteen years ago, and we have been implementing, reflecting, and revising it in all its iterations.

In the years that have passed since our initial meeting as hopeful doctoral students, we have seen huge changes and challenges in our personal lives and in our teaching. What is more, there have been even greater changes in the contexts that surround us. Our global community, for example, has suffered from unprecedented natural disasters and unparalleled political division. The world is rapidly fluctuating; the effects of a global pandemic and climate change are indicative of the urgent changes needed in schools at this time. Now, more than ever, change is needed at all levels of educational decision-making. We believe that a radical, co-collaborative, and student-centered approach to curriculum is the only way to challenge the institutionalized power of curricula across the United States. We need more than just reform—we require a fundamentally new understanding of how to better serve the ever-shifting needs of students and communities through shared responsibility for—and ownership of—what teaching and learning occurs in our classrooms at every level.

This ideological and practical shift is appropriate and necessary to our current time and place. We are calling for transformation in the creation and implementation of curricula that engages teachers, students, and communities, starting with a critical lens that asks whose interests are being served and whose needs are being ignored or subjugated. Furthermore, we believe that teacher educators and K–12 teachers can use the energy of current social movements and critical global issues as an impetus to build curriculum from the bottom up. We hope that this book becomes a springboard for teachers who will use informed decision-making. Our goal is to inspire and empower teachers to work with their students and communities to create relevant feminist, global, and anti-racist curriculum that takes into consideration local contexts and student demographics.

ORGANIZATION OF THE BOOK

This book is to be practical and applicable while also attending to theory, because teachers must be able to articulate why they do the work they do, especially when there is the possibility of resistance and upheaval. We also recognize that understanding this work is often anecdotal in nature, so each chapter will include narrative elements as well. In some ways, then, while this book addresses the *how to*, it also does so in a way that analyzes the *why, for whom*, and *with whom*. With an open mind and open heart, we also want to collaborate with you, the reader, to encourage you in the hope of moving forward as you consider a brighter, more equitable future.

In chapter 1, we share the theoretical concept of critical literacy and explicate our understanding of promoting "knowledge-in-action" through curricular conversations. We look specifically at the intersection of these two conceptual frameworks in order to show how the space created at this juncture can become a place for meaningful discourse in a classroom facilitated by both teachers and their students. We introduce Applebee's (1996) theory of curriculum as conversation and explicate the significance of Lewison, Leland, and Harste's (2011) four stances for shining a critical lens on curricular planning and content delivery. We also look at Milner's (2010) framework that covers five interconnected areas that are significant in helping educators shed light and bridge opportunity gaps that currently exist in our educational institutions.

In chapter 2, we consider the ways in which our Critical Conversations Curriculum Chart (CCCC) can assist teachers in conceiving of and planning for critical curricular conversations that can span an entire academic year. Specifically, we walk the reader through an example of a chart and discuss the ways in which an overarching question can become the basis for developing an integrated unit that prioritizes the needs, interests, and lived experiences of all the learners in their classrooms.

In chapters 3, 4, and 5 we showcase the many ways critical literacy lessons can be developed: through thematic unit planning, in disciplinary coursework, through personal and cultural resources, and with a global mindset brought to the learning situation by teachers, students, and the wider learning community. We share our experiences as teacher educators in our post-secondary classrooms, but we also provide examples of how our students—future or practicing teachers—have utilized these ideas to conceptualize their own teaching at certain grade levels or in specific content areas. While we introduce a blueprint for how we have helped our students to conceive of and plan for critical literacy lessons, we caution the reader that this outline or plan is not presented as an infallible design for developing the perfect lesson or unit. The conversations that occur in the individual classroom, the demographics of the students we teach, and the concerns and interests of our students are driving forces for our lesson planning. That is to say that while teachers can plan or prepare for critical literacy, the organic nature of both the conversation and critical literacy itself should not be compromised by strict regimens, routines, schedules, or presupposed objectives.

Chapters 6 and 7 take a deep dive into the difficulties that are often encountered by educators who wish to embrace a critical literacy/curricular conversation orientation. The very nature of standardized educational practices and the process of lesson planning remain at odds with what we are promoting when we plan for critically literate conversations in our classrooms. Standardization implies transmission-orientated educational practices in which "knowledge" and "skills" are stable and determined entities for which all students are competing. Learning, in such situations, becomes a receptive activity rather than an active, meaning-making process where knowledge is generated in relationship with others through shared activities, experimentation, and evocative classroom discourse.

In these last two chapters, we look at what it might mean for individual educators or collective professionals to move toward an equity-oriented curriculum. We consider the importance of sharing the power for curricular planning with our students and what types of inequity might be overcome by empowering ourselves and our students. We revisit what it means to plan for, develop, and implement literacy learning that rejects color blindness, deficit mindsets, and meritocracy while concurrently emphasizing the powerful role of culture and context.

In summary, in this book, we focus on three important areas that we believe are crucial for vesting teachers and students in their own equity-focused teaching and learning: (1) curricular conversations, (2) critical literacy, and (3) the sharing of power. Whether they recognize it or not, individual teachers play a powerful role in the shaping of curricula, and they do so at every level: in the planning of their lessons, in the manner in which those lessons are implemented, and in the way they allow their students to receive, react, and *interact* with the content and ideas. While we may believe that we are at the mercy of standardized educational practices and institutions, teachers *can* make a difference even when they are operating in schools and structures that do not seem to support them! We are hopeful teacher educators who embrace the belief that teachers make a difference! As part of this hope, we offer this book with its suggestions, ideas, and strategies to every teacher educator, teacher candidate, and practicing teacher as a space to consider their role in transformative education!

Chapter 1

The Intersection of Critical Literacy and Curricular Conversations

Conceiving of Social Justice

Are you skilled at seeing the big picture, focusing on the future outcome, or are you more of a detail person, paying precise attention to smaller components and features? There are benefits and limitations to both, but regarding education, Maxine Greene suggests a narrow lens has been harmful to schools and the students they serve:

> The vision that sees things "small" looks at schooling through the lenses of a system—a vantage point of power or existing ideologies—taking a primarily technical point of view. Most frequently these days it uses the lenses of benevolent policy making, with the underlying conviction that changes in schools can bring about progressive social change. . . . Whatever the precise vantage point, seeing schooling small is preoccupied with test scores, "time on task," management procedures, ethnic and racial percentages, and accountability measures, while it screens out faces and gestures of individuals, of actual living persons. (Greene, 1995, p. 11)

There are popular expressions that are used when somebody gets so caught up in specifics that it impacts how well they can see the whole picture. They are "getting caught in the weeds" or may "be unable to see the forest because of the trees." One gets so concerned with the small details that it prevents them from understanding what is important. Greene (1995) explains that this often occurs in the field of education, drawing our attention to processes and procedures over people. It is, perhaps, an easier view to have in education, attending to specific and objective tasks rather than addressing the complications brought by actual students and the messy, unjust world in which they live.

Consequently, in this chapter, we begin to explore what it means to conceive of justice and how we, as educators, can go about creating classrooms that embrace a justice-oriented curriculum by looking at the intersection of critical literacy and curricular conversations. In order to begin the work of developing a justice-centered curriculum, we must take a step back from the day-to-day or lesson-to-lesson planning and adopt a wider lens, a "big picture" view.

THE DISTRACTION OF THE "SMALL"

The quote above by Maxine Greene is thought-provoking because what stands out first and foremost is the idea that "benevolent" policy making can somehow, magically, lead to "progressive social change." It implies that, like White foster parents Leigh Anne and Sean Tuohy Greene who swooped in to save an undereducated and impoverished Black Michael Oher in *The Blind Side* (2009), well-intentioned educators can produce educational and social change through the implementation of compassionate educational policies and procedures. It also suggests that any ideas, thoughts, and plans the receivers of this "benevolent" gesture may have for their own future are not considered because the institution understands what is best for its members. While we understand the aim of such thinking, intentionality does not necessarily produce the results we desire.

Like Greene, we believe that benevolence has very little, if anything, to do with progressive social change in classrooms or in the development of a justice-oriented educational perspective. Progressive social change rarely begins at the top, because the top prioritizes the voices of those in power, those whose interests are being served by maintaining the status quo. Instead, we believe that true educational and social reform occurs from the bottom up, in the teaching trenches, so to speak, when those without the power begin asking why their voices and needs are being ignored, and they begin to resist.

The second thing that stands out is the concept of keeping things "small" and technical in nature. Keeping things "small" discourages a big-picture perspective and a wider lens where individuals both within the system and outside of it can see the interrelated dynamics and can come to understand why things are the way they are. Unfortunately, systemic education is full of "small" things and "small" ideas that are founded in a powerful network of White, male, colonialist histories. From the lists of historical dates or mathematical facts to be memorized to individual and daily lesson plans to summative assessments reported on grade cards at the end of a term, educators rarely have the time, opportunity, or experience to evaluate their work from a broader perspective, apart from the occasional reflexivity of considering whether or not their instruction is leading to student learning.

Keeping things "small" also means that teacher educators teach preservice educators the ways of teaching by introducing them to the varied aspects of what it means to teach in manageable soundbites. This represents the difference between training and educating. Teacher educators require preservice teachers to master disciplinary content or write lesson objectives in separate and discrete ways. As a result, students in teacher colleges simply build on what they have learned in their liberal arts and content foundation courses and begin learning the processes and procedures believed to be effective in teaching that content to their own students. The "faces and gestures" of their future students are intentionally obscured (save for the cursory nod to the importance of "activating prior knowledge" of those students) in order to focus on the more tangible and concrete.

Both teacher candidates and practicing educators spend a great deal of time learning how to design detailed lesson plans by writing learning objectives, choosing appropriate materials and activities, and connecting these to assessments that are supposed to determine whether or not student learning has occurred. Beyond this, educators are provided very little direction in conceiving of how these individual lesson plans might fit together beyond a single skills lesson or a simple unit plan. What is more, very few opportunities are provided for teachers to consider whether these lessons are relevant to their students' lived experiences or how these lessons might be perceived by the students they teach.

This "smallness" in teaching can lead to a diminutive perspective of both student and teacher potential. Rather than seeing all manner of possibilities in the acts of teaching and learning, they are reduced to transmission-oriented instruction. Knowledge becomes stable and predetermined, an entity for which everyone in the classroom is competing. It presupposes that there is something all of us "need" to know and creates a dynamic where the students are required to absorb, memorize, and master information that the teacher explicitly and directly disseminates. Learning becomes a receptive activity, rather than an interactive or transactive one, and eliminates the need for student engagement, active meaning-making, and construction of a common understanding.

In order to negate this smallness and create a larger vision, we must begin to see all manner of possibilities in the world. As Greene (1995) indicated, "we acknowledge the harshness of situations only when we have in mind another state of affairs in which things would be better" (p. ix). It is in this space that we challenge ourselves and our students to look beyond traditional, taken-for-granted ways of teaching and learning. After decades in the field, challenging ourselves can be difficult and even scary. Nevertheless, we embrace a hopeful vision that deconstructs the current system of institutionalized power and existing ideologies of curricula and attempts to serve the needs of students and communities through shared responsibility and ownership for the curricula that is utilized in classrooms.

Knowing whether you are a detail-oriented or big-picture-oriented individual is critical. As we have indicated, both have their advantages and disadvantages. For the purpose of long-term planning, however, finding ways to prioritize the big picture will allow you to develop the skills and strategies necessary to develop that overall sense of purpose and direction that hopeful educators need in order to ensure that their students understand where they are going and why. Students are better able to successfully enter a classroom conversation when the connections are made explicit in clear and transparent ways.

TEXTBOX 1.1. MOMENT OF REFLECTION: DO *I* GET "STUCK IN THE WEEDS"?

In order to ascertain if you are skilled at seeing the big picture and focusing on the future outcome, or if are you more of a detail person who pays particular attention to smaller mechanisms and structures, let's engage in a short role play. Pretend you are volunteering at an animal shelter where you are learning your role and responsibilities.

When you enter the facility, (1) do you take a good look around and get a "lay of the land" by surveying the overall structure and design of the facility? Or (2) do you go immediately to the front desk, introduce yourself, and request to see the person in charge so that they can explain what you will be doing?

When going to your first scheduled appointment to volunteer, (1) do you see what jobs and tasks others are fulfilling to get a sense of how your job is related and "fits in" to the overall care of the animals? Or (2) do you concentrate solely on your role with the animals as indicated by your job description?

When working directly with the animals, (1) do you attempt to learn as much as possible about the animal by seeking out information about the background, history, and preferences? Or (2) do you walk in the animal stall and complete the tasks you've been given?

IS THERE A WAY FOR TEACHERS TO PRIORITIZE THE "BIG PICTURE" AND AVOID THE "DISTRACTION OF THE SMALL"?

While there are multiple ways of conceiving of curriculum, we choose to utilize Applebee's (1996) theory of "curriculum as conversation." In our doctoral studies, we were introduced to Arthur Applebee and found his theory to be a useful way to conceptualize and prioritize "classroom talk." We believe that viewing curricula less as a set of standards and more as an overarching sense of purpose and direction allows teachers to challenge the transmission-oriented instructional design that direct and explicit teaching methodology embraces. It places a focus, instead, on the types of conversations that emerge in the classroom during instruction. Although traditions of discourse within real-world disciplines are in a continuous state of change and evolution, what students often learn in schools is usually static. Instead of vibrant classroom dialogue, children are forced to engage in the distilled and codified notions of disciplinary traditions that once existed or exist still, but only in "the real world."

Consequently, many curricula present "knowledge-out-of-context," requiring students to learn *about* disembodied content that is detached from its original purpose or practice in the larger, disciplinary community. A decontextualized curriculum "may enable students to do well on multiple choice items . . . [but] it does not enable them to enter on their own into our vital academic traditions of knowing and doing" (Applebee, 1996, p. 33). The content in such a curriculum does not induce student participation or encourage the development of further conversations across time and disciplinary boundaries. Any teacher who has ever had to consider standardized tests their students may take will certainly understand the dilemma that teachers face when they are expected to teach lists of facts, dates, or skills without time or consideration for their larger context or real-world purpose. It stands in direct opposition to Applebee's (1996) notion of a curriculum of "knowledge-in-action" that encourages students to enter current conversations within living traditions of disciplinary discourse.

What is more, Applebee's (1996) conception of curriculum is also useful for our purposes in that he identifies five curricular structures (see table 1.1). These structures are organized on a continuum according to the extent to which they encourage or discourage the expansion of engaging disciplinary conversations in the classroom. The structures include catalog, collection, sequential, episodic, and integrated curricula. In order to understand our emphasis on integrated curricular, the following offers a brief synopsis of his curricular structures.

Table 1.1. Arthur Applebee's Curricular Structures

Type of Curriculum	Definition	Example(s)
Catalog	Listing of items or experiences with no link among the parts	Literature chosen at random, perhaps based on readability or availability of texts
Collection	Identifying a topic and choosing elements to explore based on a sense of "set-ness"	Literature studies where students sample genres like poems or science fiction, or read several books by the same author
Sequential	Collections that have an internal order based on chronology or hierarchy	American literature in sequence from colonial works to the early 1900s
Episodic	Sequential curriculum with a stronger sense of overall topics	American literature as a reflection of the politics and culture of the time
Integrated	Independent but interacting experiences; can discover interrelationships across all elements so that the parallel but independent discussions of an episodic curriculum begin to echo back on one another	A world cultures course where students study different cultures episodically, but use it as a basis to have conversations about multiculturalism, traditions, perspectives, and various literary patterns as represented across the cultures studied

Curricula that *catalog* materials, events, or experiences present these as discrete and separate, with no overarching domain for conversation. Despite the fact that this type of curriculum fails to support classroom discourse beyond a single content lesson or skill, Applebee indicates that these are surprisingly common in classrooms. A *collection* provides for both the teacher and students a sense of "set-ness," where a variety of texts are sampled, skills are taught, or content disseminated in relationship to one another. Once this "set" has been covered, the teacher and students move on to the next isolated set. This structure allows for conversation about the relationship among the individual elements of the set, but it does not explore the interconnectedness of the sets themselves.

When a sense of chronology is added to a collection, the result is a *sequential* curricular construction. While such a curriculum has an inherent and logical order, the result is that "the elements sit in a fixed and relatively narrow relationship to one another" (p. 74), leaving very few opportunities for a conversation to develop about how these components relate to one another. Often students do not even recognize the chronological structure of their curricula. If a clearer sense of an overall topic or theme is affixed to a sequential curriculum, the structure becomes *episodic*. In such a curriculum, students are encouraged to return at standard intervals (e.g., at the end of a unit) to the overarching theme so that students can explore the basic principle as it applies to each new element.

The most inclusive and comprehensive curricular structure is the *integrated* curriculum. Because most fields of study are not neat, tidy, and orderly, multiple conversations usually emerge with the relationship between and among them as important as the individual conversations themselves. This is a curriculum that is comprised of "independent but interacting experiences" (Applebee, 1996, p. 77), which allows for students to not only explore the overarching topic itself but also to reflect perspectives that the newly introduced elements provide. Integrated curricula allow for continuing and recurring conversations that provide opportunities to return to earlier material in the light of new considerations and echo back on information previously encountered. As a result, students' understanding is both broadened and deepened simultaneously, encouraging disciplinary conversations that are personally, culturally, and pedagogically relevant to both the teacher and their students.

Applebee (1996) argued that conceiving of curricula as "domains for culturally significant conversations" can provide a way of conceiving curriculum as more than just *what* is learned, but *how* it is learned as well. This is perhaps even more critical now than ever. There is an abundance of information confronting students regularly from a variety of sources: the internet, social media, news outlets, family dialogue, local events, cultural patterns, textbooks, peers, and so on. Each of these informational sources carries its own disciplinary discourses, often with conflicting ideologies and purposes. Allowing students the opportunity to weave knowledge from varied perspectives provides a wider lens for critical analysis. Curricula, then, become the organic and dynamic conversations around which all texts, classroom discussions, and pedagogical activities are centered (Applebee, 2002). As such, *integrated* instruction creates spaces for students to explore, investigate, and consider all manner of interpretive possibilities (Applebee, 1997), making the classroom a hopeful and transformative space.

We also recognize that curricula in which students are drawn into the domains of culturally significant conversation are inherently more engaging because students can incorporate contemporary issues and student concerns; culturally significant conversations value and prioritize the shared dialogue of teacher and student. When students are given an opportunity to contribute to the development of curriculum through "classroom talk," they are also empowered to take ownership of their own learning, generating both enthusiasm and interest. In this way, we encourage teachers to allow students to learn *how* to think, not *what* to think.

WHY ADD CRITICAL LITERACY TO
THIS INTEGRATED UNIT PLAN?

Like integrated instruction and curricular conversations that can occur in classrooms, critical literacy is fundamentally engaging because it encourages readers to use their own power to construct understanding and negotiate the author's intentions. Critical literacy encourages students to examine texts in order to understand the relationship between language and power. Critical literacy positions learners in ways that allow them to question, analyze, resist, and act upon injustices and oppressions; it requires students to consciously engage, take responsibility for inquiry, be reflective, and entertain alternative ways of being (Lewison, Leland, & Harste, 2011).

Critical literacy is transformative in nature both by its definition and in its practice. Critical literacy rejects the tenets of essentialism; it is antipositivist, rejecting the idea that there exists an "objective approach to classroom contexts and discourses" (Giroux, 1992) that all teachers *must* follow in order to be effective. Contrary to structuralist theories of reproduction where students are rewarded for how well they "do school," transformative theories of education like critical literacy suggest that schools are ideal sites for promoting social change. As a result, we endorse curricula that focuses on social critique leading to change (Freire & Macedo, 1987; Giroux, 1992). This is to say that it is important that teachers view schools as places of hopeful change—not neutral sites where objective knowledge is transferred from teacher to student regardless of social or cultural locations and identities. As hopeful educators, we see the sociocultural implications of knowledge production and the transfer of knowledge as evident in *all* teaching and learning endeavors.

When engaging in a critical pedagogy (out of which critical literacy has grown), an educator can make students' social problems and the conditions lived by students visible. In this way, educators and students interact to discern and address such problems in pedagogical and political terms within the school context. McLaren (2000) suggests that Freire's work is essential to the progressive advancement of educational thought because the future of education is intimately connected to the increased ability of students *and* teachers to become critically self-reflective. Consequently, educators and students alike are called to differentiate and analyze the ways in which their own gendered, racialized, and sexualized experiences have been inscribed through limiting discursive practices and material social relations that support powerful, elite groups at the expense of most of the population.

WHY DOES ANY OF THIS MATTER?

It is exciting to consider the fact that English Language Arts (ELA) educators who strive to develop students' critical literacy can provide a basis for creating very real social change from the bottom up! By focusing on contemporary social issues and students' lived experiences, we bring into focus *who* engages in *what*, in *what context*, and for *what purpose*. This moves us farther away from the "smallness" of traditional teaching and allows us a "big picture" perspective. As Lewis (2001) claimed, "We cannot separate literacy, and the cognition involved in literacy, from affect, from society, from culture, or from politics in the sense of equal and fair access to social participation and power" (p. xviii). In this way, literacy can and should be viewed as communicative competence in particular contexts rather than the simple mastery of an isolated set of skills.

Critical literacy is "a politics of thinking from the margins, of possessing integral perspectives on the world" (Lankshear & McLaren, 1993, p. 27). As a result, ELA educators and their students can understand the world through who they are and what they know using critical literacy pedagogy. With a Freirean lens or perspective, people can approach the historical and cultural world as a transformable reality, continuously shaped by hopeful humans.

In our courses and in our research, we have utilized Lewison, Leland, and Harste's (2011) model of critical literacy instruction because it articulates, among other things, the importance of defining such instruction as a "transaction" like Applebee's emphasis on *knowledge-in-action*. Such a transaction involves movement and interaction among the personal and cultural resources individuals use, the critical social practices they enact, and the critical stances that individuals adopt in both the classroom and the world. The transactional pedagogical model allows us to conceptualize our teaching from a big-picture perspective. It helps us keep in focus our larger literacy practices (i.e., How will we engage in classroom discourse? What texts will we require students to consume and produce?). It helps us to encourage, maintain, and balance participation from both the student and the teacher and to challenge our understanding and acceptance of the power structures that support and test our work as both educator and learner in and outside of our classrooms.

While it is challenging, we, as teachers, can prepare for critical literacy by helping students take a critical stance and providing them access to resources. Taking a critical stance involves encouraging them to consciously engage with not only the content but also one another, requiring them to entertain alternative ways of thinking and being, allowing them to take responsibility for inquiry, and providing time and opportunity for ongoing reflection. Resources can and should be wide and varied and may include personal

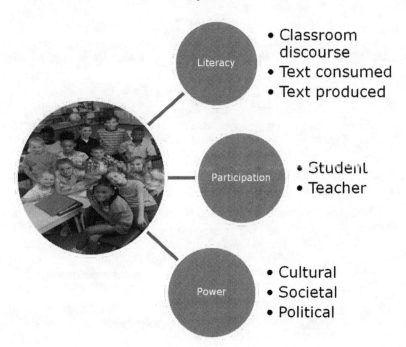

- Classroom discourse
- Text consumed
- Text produced

- Student
- Teacher

- Cultural
- Societal
- Political

Figure 1.1. Pedagogical Model of Critical Literacy Instruction

experiences, popular culture, media, social-issue texts, textbooks, critical books, oral texts, oral histories, community concerns, societal issues, and even personal desires, interests, or needs. The fuel for those critical conversations can be found all around us!

As students and teachers work together to create critical curricula in real time in real classrooms from the bottom up, they engage in four specific dimensions of social practice:

1. *They disrupt the commonplace.* Teachers and students examine how social norms are communicated and propagated through popular culture including media and texts, allowing students to interrogate their taken-for-granted understandings of how their world works and why it works the way that it does.
2. *They consider multiple viewpoints.* Teachers and students are challenged to step outside themselves and their own perspectives in order to consider and appreciate multiple realities, giving a voice to those who have been silenced or marginalized, or making spaces for those voices. This is especially important in our current political climate, where individuals have a tendency to operate in echo chambers that ignore, discount, or disregard differing ideas or contradictory possibilities.

3. *They focus on the sociopolitical.* Teachers and students analyze the relationship between language and power with the intent of deconstructing and then reconstructing the ways in which language is used to maintain dominance and the status quo. This analysis includes the consideration of what language systems are prioritized and which are disregarded.
4. *They take action to promote social justice.* Critical literacy requires that teachers and students answer the call for becoming actors in the world rather than spectators (Freire, 1970). Together, they find myriad ways to get messages of democracy, justice, and equity out into the world.

DOES MOVING TOWARD JUSTICE AND EQUITY REALLY MATTER FOR ME AND MY STUDENTS?

The time is ripe for these messages of democracy, justice, and equity. Currently, there are multiple ongoing conversations within specific disciplines and in schooling at large that indicate we are at a crossroads. One such example is the recent upsurge of legislation that seeks to silence some voices, such as Florida's HB 1557 that has banned public school teachers from introducing texts or engaging in classroom instruction about sexual orientation or gender identity "in a manner that is not age-appropriate or developmentally appropriate for students in accordance with state standards." Another more prevalent example is the fact that inequitable access to education and lack of resources became even more noticeable during the pandemic, highlighting the ways in which the educational system is oppressive rather than liberatory, especially for BIPOC students and teachers, based in economic injustice and inequity.

According to Gorski (2018), almost 31 million children in the US are experiencing poverty and 5 percent live in deep poverty, meaning the family income is less than half the federal poverty line. This is more problematic when one considers how those in poverty are viewed. Using a deficit ideology, the pervasive view in the US, poverty is viewed as a symptom of ethical, dispositional, and even spiritual deficiencies in the individuals and communities experiencing it. Using a structural ideology, one recognizes that the disparity is caused by logical and unjust outcomes of economic injustice and inequity. Consequently, Gorski (2018) defines equity literacy as the "knowledge and skills educators need to become a threat to the existence of bias and inequity in our spheres of influence" (p. 17). He claims that while teachers grow their knowledge (developing bigger understandings, strengthening abilities to recognize the inequities students experience in and out of schools and how those inequities impact their school engagement) and the skills (cultivating abilities to act for equity, to advocate, to prioritize the educational success of students experiencing the most inequity by reshaping policy and practice), rarely do they move to the final step, which is the will to act.

Embedding critical literacies into an integrated curriculum and sharing power with students and the communities in which schools are embedded is one way to work for equity and justice at the base. To clarify, it is not just classroom work, but *world* work—that is, *knowledge-in-action*. One learns and reflects, thereby developing the critical dispositions, skills, and abilities required to act.

As those who have worked in the field of education and been, at times, complicit in the inequities reinforced there, we recognize "that public education, though a noble ideal, rather than 'level the playing field,' often served instead to exacerbate inequalities, particularly around race, ethnicity, social class, language, and other differences" (Nieto, 2017, pp. 23–24). We believe that due to the "the enduring presence of institutional racism and the culture of whiteness in the academy" (Picower & Kohli, 2017, p. 6) and throughout K–12 schooling, there is radical work to be done in schools and in teacher education programs. We need to "disrupt the discourse in the larger teacher educational spaces that normalized whiteness, White supremacy, and class hostility toward urban youth and youth of Color" (Camangian, 2017, p. 32). Understanding the discourses and ongoing conversations, identifying who has access, and clarifying how they intersect are critical steps in being able to disrupt them.

There are numerous contradictions (as they relate to class, gender, ethnicity, sexuality, nationality, and ability) vying for space and discourse in every classroom, regardless of the discipline. As educators, how we self-identify, the critical stance we develop, and the critical practices in which we engage, will not only shape our experiences but also the experiences of our students and readers. But as educators committed to equity and justice, what choice do we have?

The current conversations of abolitionist teaching means allowing this focus on equity and justice to permeate all aspects of our work and our lives. It could include the following radical moves:

> Reimagining and rewriting curriculums with local and national activists to provide students with not only examples of resistance but also strategies of resistance. Protecting and standing in solidarity with immigrant children and their families. Joining pro-immigrant community organizations in the fight for rights for all. Knowing that freedom is impossible without women and queer leaders being the thinkers and doers of abolitionist movements. (Love, 2020, p. 11)

This critical work is about being immersed in the changes we want to see and taking action as a part of something larger and for the greater good in the name of equity and justice.

HOPEFUL TEACHERS MOVE TOWARD
JUSTICE AND EQUITY

In this text, we have chosen to utilize Milner's (2010) Diversity and Opportunity Gaps Explanatory Framework to organize our thinking about pedagogical action that must be taken to behave in ways that will create the change we want to see. In this framework, Milner delineates five interconnected areas that are critical in helping educators shed light on and bridge opportunity gaps for the purpose of promoting equity in education: (1) the rejection of colorblindness; (2) the development of skills to understand, work through, and transcend cultural conflicts; (3) overcoming the myth of meritocracy; (4) the denunciation of deficit mindsets; and (5) the resistance of context-neutral mindsets and practices. The table below (table 1.2) identifies

Table 1.2. Milner's Diversity and Opportunity Gaps Framework

Areas That Can Bridge Opportunity Gaps	Definition	Hopeful Teachers Should
Colorblindness	Persistent notion that race, and how race operates, has no bearing at the individual or system levels of education	Challenge themselves to understand how race-centered experiences shape our attitudes, beliefs, and ideologies both in and out of the classroom
Cultural conflicts	Conflicts that emerge as a result of the cultural experiences of both teachers and students	Be mindful of how an educator's cultural ways of knowing often subordinate and diminish their students' cultural ways of knowing in a classroom
Meritocracy	The belief that student performance is a function of hard work, ability, skill, intelligence, and persistence	Make themselves cognizant of the fact that situations far beyond a student's (or parents') control can affect academic and social success at school
Deficit mindsets	A focus on what students do not have or do not bring to the classroom	Set high expectations for all children and consider the many funds of knowledge that students bring to learning opportunities in the classroom
Context-neutral mindsets	A belief that the contexts that surround teaching (state, city, and local governments, ideology of the school, political movements) have no bearing on the learning that occurs in schools	Keep abreast of contextual complexity in which schools are situated and recognize that how the world works and how education works can create a disadvantage for many students

these five areas, their definitions, and the ways in which attending to them can close opportunity gaps.

Reject Colorblindness

Using critical literacy in an integrated curriculum, educators are empowered to challenge persistent notions that they should avoid the recognition of race and how race operates on both the individual and systemic levels in educational institutions. Educators are encouraged to plan for and engage in ongoing conversations that acknowledge the ways in which race-central experiences shape understandings, attitudes, belief systems, principles, and eventually our actions and practices. The rejection of colorblindness allows educators to understand that, in both theory and praxis, *race matters* in both society and in the classroom. The intersection of critical literacy in curricular conversation provides a safe space for both teachers and students to question, analyze, resist, and act upon injustice and oppression.

Transcend Cultural Conflicts

Cultural conflicts can cause incongruence between teachers and learners, making teaching and learning difficult or even impossible. Teachers may recognize the need for cultural awareness or have the desire to become culturally competent but find it difficult to shake their Eurocentric ideologies and ideals. Critical literacy practices allow both educators and students to consciously engage with one another and entertain alternative ways of being, creating a deeper understanding of the role that culture plays in curriculum development, educational decision-making, and classroom discourses. This can lead to the sharing of power, which is critical to the promotion of justice- and equity-based educational processes.

Confront the Myth of Meritocracy

Many educators, based on their own educational background and life experiences, have adopted a lens of meritocracy. This is to say that they believe that student success is primarily the result of hard work, ability, intelligence, skill, and tenacity, and, as a result, the lack of success in educational settings is a student's (or their family's) failure or shortcoming in those same areas. An integrated curriculum infused with critical literacy confronts this particularly harmful ideology, requiring educators to acknowledge and address the fact that there are many aspects of our lived experiences that shape both academic and social success. It requires both teachers and students to be reflective and analyze the systems of oppression that operate in schools and in society as a whole.

Denounce Deficit Mindsets

It is not uncommon for educators to have low expectations of particular students, specifically BIPOC communities suffering poverty. These deficit mindsets become their own self-fulfilling prophesies, where students rise only to the level set or anticipated. With a deficit mindset, educators focus on what skills, knowledge, or experiences a student is lacking and cannot or does not bring to the classroom. By its very nature, critical literacy uses as a starting point the understanding, knowledge, and areas of interest or concern a student brings to any classroom conversation, honoring their personal funds of knowledge. Moreover, it affords students the opportunity to consciously engage and take responsibility for their own learning. It allows for the sharing of power in which students are not only encouraged but also required to question, analyze, reflect, plan, and act.

Resist Context-Neutral Mindsets

Teaching and learning never take place in a vacuum, devoid of distinctions and nuances that make it unique. Despite our best efforts to welcome all our students and create an impartial and neutral environment, there are contexts that surround our teaching at every level. From the background of the teacher to the culture of the school and leadership of the administration, to the local community, to state and national atmosphere and political temperature, social contexts affect both teaching and learning. By understanding and acknowledging the ways in which these contexts influence how the world works and how education works, teachers can empower students to take a closer look at the systems of power that are at work and to confront and resist these. Critical literacy requires such investigation and action.

Embedding critical literacies into an integrated curriculum provides a range of opportunities for sharing power with students, parents, and the communities in which schools exist. Our goal is to help educators begin the world-work in the context of their own classrooms by teaching themselves and their students to become reflective, develop critical dispositions, and take responsibility to question and to act. As Gorski (2018) indicates,

> Our first role as equity literature educators is to identify all the ways this opportunity is not equitably distributed within our spheres of influence. Perhaps your sphere of influence is a classroom. Developing equity literacy will help you identify the equity gaps, the opportunity gaps . . . by strengthening your ability to recognize them. It also will give you the skills to eliminate ways you might unintentionally perpetuate those gaps in your classroom. (p. 26)

Moving toward equity-based educational philosophy and practice is not about creating an appearance of being fair and impartial but, rather, about drawing attention to and removing barriers to opportunity. In utilizing critical literacy, we allow for students from different racial, ethnic, and cultural backgrounds to maximize the assets they bring to the classroom. An integrated curricular structure emphasizes and utilizes the knowledge-in-action that both teachers and their students will engage in in larger contexts. As Milner suggests, "All students and teachers deserve to be engaged in opportunities that can improve their own lives and those of others as they work to make meaningful contributions to their families, their communities, and to society" (Milner, 2010, p. 8).

UNDERSTANDING THE STRUCTURE OF THIS TEXT

In the next five chapters, we will introduce Critical Conversations Curriculum Charts (CCCC) and guide the reader through their intended purpose, structure, and possibilities. These chapters are not meant to be used as a prescriptive "how-to." The goal is for teacher candidates and practicing educators to consider how the CCCC, in conjunction with their students' needs, interests, and experiences, can help educators plan for transformative pedagogy. As such, it is our hope that educators who read this text will understand that curricula are dynamic, emerging out of the transactions, interactions, and discourses that occur in an ever-changing classroom.

The chapters are designed to resist and counter the distraction of the small. Like the CCCC themselves, each chapter starts with an overarching question, intended to emphasize the "big picture" for the reader. Likewise, the big ideas that follow are meant to bring into focus the larger ideas that provide a basis for future consideration, reflection, or integration. We provide samples and lessons or units, make suggestions where applicable, and finally, consider the ways in which these ideas deconstruct the current system of institutionalized power and push the boundaries for shared control and authority over curricula and classroom conversations. We leave you with a parting thought to consider as you move forward. It is our hope that, as you read, you begin to consider the many ways you can create a hopeful, transformative classroom space for all of your students.

Chapter 2

Critical Conversations Curriculum Charts

Intersection of Curriculum as Conversation and Critical Literacy as Transformative Space

Overarching question: What possibilities exist at the intersection of curriculum as conversation and critical literacy?

Big Ideas:

- "Talk" in the form of classroom discourse is central to the development of curricula in real time.
- Curricula exist at three levels: what is planned by the teacher, what is enacted in the classroom, and what is received by students.
- While it is important to plan for classroom discourse, teachers must be both disciplined and flexible enough to allow for emerging conversations.

THE IMPORTANCE OF TALK

The use of talk is crucial to the intersection of curriculum as conversation and critical literacy that we endorse in this text. Talk is at the heart of what we do when we teach and when we learn. The words we choose to use when we present information, the texts we choose to read or assign, the texts we expect students to produce, the assignments we anticipate they will complete, and the manner in which we listen and engage with our students' talk all matter. Shor (1999) states that "we are what we say and do. The way we speak and are spoken to help shape us into the people we become" (p. 1) both in and outside of the classroom. It is critical that teachers consider not only *what* they will teach, but *how*—the manner in which they will engage their students in conversations about that content use talk.

Language is the heart of developing and implementing a curriculum of conversation, not only in the discourse encouraged within the classroom context but also in the language of texts chosen to represent that curriculum. Language makes up the texts that students will consume and those that they will produce. Curricula are dependent on the very tool necessary for engaging in critical literacy the tool of language. What is more, we must remember that the consumption and production of texts, response activities, and all subsequent conversations in a classroom are socially situated (Gallas & Smagorinsky, 2002). All pedagogical practices, then, including the talk that is undertaken by the teacher and her students will either encourage or discourage the various connections that students will make to the content, the texts, and the conversations themselves. Applebee (1997) reminds us that "classroom conversations gain their educational power because they take place in a context shaped by the larger discourse communities of which they are a part. In entering a classroom conversation, participants are learning the rules of discourse of the larger community as well" (p. 27). It is for that reason we emphasize that classroom talk has to be purposefully planned and organized, yet flexible enough to allow space for it to be dynamic, transformative, and collaborative.

Talk plays a decisive role in the implementation and mediation of critical literacy within the classroom context. Lewison, Leland, and Harste (2011) posit that there are attitudes and dispositions we adopt that enable us to become critically literate beings. Taking a critical stance shapes language, even as the talk in which we engage outlines and illuminates our critical positions. Language is how we bridge the personal and the social. A simple example of movement between the personal and social is the expression of our wants and needs. Our needs, which can be described as personal, are made social when we verbalize them. Thus, moving between the social and the personal is an important aspect of what teachers do in the classroom that allows their students to engage, interact, and become invested in the content we teach.

The Critical Conversations Curriculum Chart (CCCC) that we propose and utilize here was first conceived and introduced in the context of our methods courses as teacher educators. It emphasizes, in both content and structure, the importance of the talk we generate in the classroom. It considers the ways in which the questions posed by teachers, supported by the texts they choose and the assignments they require, support classroom discourse around relevant and engaging topics. It is useful in helping teachers consider and manage the many conversations that will (and should) emerge as new material is introduced and layered upon existing information and knowledge in an integrated curriculum.

We perceive the CCCC as different from curriculum mapping even though it could be used in tandem with that process. Specifically, the CCCC provides an external structure and framework, while traditional curriculum maps suggest an internal structure. Traditional mapping has, as its main purpose, the provision of measurable improvement in targeted student performance areas and, as a process of ongoing curriculum and assessment review, curriculum mapping often begins with a graded course of study, a content standard, or a specific learning objective. Because its prime objective is to collect curricular operational data that leads to student assessment and evaluation (Jacobs, 2004), curriculum mapping is often associated with skills and content that often remain disconnected from students' areas of interest, concern, and background knowledge.

Conversely, the CCCC, modeled after Applebee's conceptions of an integrated curriculum and knowledge-in-action, requires teachers to contemplate the following: (1) designing a yearlong or ongoing conversation, subdivided into conversational domains that are represented by overarching questions or conversation starters; (2) choosing texts that students will engage with via reading, writing, listening, speaking, viewing, and visually representing as part of that conversation; and (3) considering how they will implement smaller units of instruction. Such instruction includes classroom discourses, lesson-specific inquiries, and assignments that focus on curricular conversations within disciplinary domains. Our objective was to create spaces whereby educators could explore, examine, and contemplate all manner of interpretive possibilities with and for their students. While some students may bring background knowledge to the ideas at hand, for example, other students may be engaging with this information or considering the content for the first time. That said, all students have lived experiences that can be brought to bear on the content and the texts, and the conversations that emerge in the classroom must be inclusive enough to allow for them.

THE LEVELS OF CURRICULUM

It has long been understood that curriculum exists at three levels: the planned, the enacted, and the received. The planned (or intended) formal curriculum includes all the lesson plans created, syllabi written, textbooks chosen, activities organized, materials gathered, and objectives determined by the teacher, the school, the district, and the state. The enacted (or implemented) curriculum involves what occurs in the classroom. The teacher's and students' interactions with and around the planned curriculum may transform the planned curriculum. Activities that have been planned, for example, may be altered once instruction has occurred. Or teachers may find a planned assessment is insufficient to evaluate what learning has taken place and decide to eliminate it. The received (or attained) curriculum reflects how students make sense of the content or curricular conversations in which they are engaged and how (or if) they adopt the skills being taught. Some students may not be aware of the intended purpose of either the planned or enacted curriculum; likewise, teachers may not be cognizant of the fact that the curriculum their students receive and perceive is not the knowledge, skills, or content that were intended.

The key to the CCCC assignment in our methods courses was that the questions produced by the teacher candidates during the unit planning were simply viewed as starting points; ultimately, their students would be provided an opportunity to take some control of the conversations in which they would engage. It was our hope that, once implemented, the students themselves would guide the direction of the classroom conversations initially planned by the teachers, creating potential for a closer connection among the planned, enacted, and received curricula. Whereas curricular mapping includes essential questions, content, skills, assessments, activities, and resources designed and implemented by the teacher with a clear trajectory and ultimate destination, the syntheses of curricular conversation theory and critical literacy pedagogy through the CCCC was intended to holistically lay the foundation for dynamic and collaborative curricular conversations. In essence, the curricular structure, though it would be initiated by the teacher through the overarching question, was meant to be driven by the students in the class, those participants in the ever-changing, ever-evolving curricular "talk." The curriculum, then, would gain momentum and lead somewhere precisely because the conversations are "real, [and, thus,] they . . . create a meaningful context for what we ask students to read and write and talk about" (Applebee, 1994, p. 50). Where these conversations would lead is ultimately unknown, meaning that the teacher would need to be flexible enough to allow for students to do independent investigative work that can be brought to the class and shared.

WHAT'S MISSING?

As Burroughs (1999) has indicated, it is insufficient to simply modify the types of texts we expect students to consume and produce in our English Language Arts classrooms for the purpose of creating change or embracing emancipatory and justice-centered curricula. We cannot simply add "critical literacy" texts or objectives to our curricula and expect transformative pedagogy to emerge. To truly transform the distilled and extracted nature of traditional classroom instruction, teachers "must challenge conventional talk about texts" (p. 137) and find new ways to invite students into an ongoing and engaging conversation in the same way those disciplinary discourses may occur outside of the classroom context. Burroughs contends that, even more important than the texts themselves, chosen to represent the teacher's idea of what constitutes appropriate literature and necessary content knowledge, is the conversation, the talk, in which those texts and that instruction are nested.

It is important that we remind the reader of our orientation to Applebee's (1996) conception of curriculum that was discussed in the first chapter. The five curricular structures that he identifies are catalog, collection, sequential, episodic, and integrated curricula. As indicated, when a clear sense of an overall topic or theme is attached to a sequential curriculum, the structure becomes episodic. This is a curricular organization where students are encouraged to return to the overarching theme in order to explore the basic principle(s) as they are applied to each newly introduced concept or idea.

Our goal, however, is to reach the most inclusive and comprehensive curricular structure—the *integrated* curriculum. As such, it is insufficient to simply tie the individual lessons to an overarching theme as is often done in a thematic unit plan or to merge content area skills introduction as is often done in interdisciplinary curricular planning. Instead, we emphasize that educators must plan for the messiness of multiple conversations within a classroom and allow for opportunities to explore the relationships between and among the emerging ideas. This should be done in as organic a way as possible, where conversations may begin to take on a life of their own. As a curriculum of "independent but interacting experiences" (p. 77), an *integrated* thematic unit encourages students to not only explore the overarching theme or topic but also to reflect the many diverse perspectives that the newly introduced elements and emerging conversations provide. It builds upon itself and leads somewhere. As we have emphasized already, this allows educators to conceive of curriculum as more than just the *what* of learning, but the *how* of learning as well.

We cannot underscore enough the importance of prioritizing *integrated* thematic instruction as the means to create spaces for teachers and learners to explore, investigate, and consider all manner of interpretive possibility that can occur as teachers and learners engage in classroom conversations. As Applebee (1996) indicates:

Most fields of study are not neat and tidy, with one dominant conversation in which everyone participates happily. Disciplines are more like societies than communities: they are built out of many different local conversations, with different histories and major participants, often in competition for status and position within the field. . . . As we think about curriculum as it plays itself out across courses and years, the relationships among such conversations become increasingly important. (p. 64)

Applebee argues against the idea of "education as one great conversation." He states that liberal and progressive educators have long sought to correlate curriculum in all fields across subject areas in an attempt to provide their students with a "unified vision of the world." The problem with this, according to Applebee, is that when we focus only on the commonalities across traditions of discourse, we lose "sight of the differences that are also part of their richness and appeal." We must, then, leave our classroom conversations open to both disciplinary and interdisciplinary discourses and attempt to balance these, considering the individuals who will be engaging in them. We must take into account the areas of interest, knowledge, and meaning that both teacher and students will bring to each and every curricular conversation, both on a daily basis and across time. In this way, we emphasize knowledge-in-action (learning that involves both knowing and doing simultaneously) over knowledge-out-of-context (learning about content in ways that are static and distilled).

The CCCC is simple but purposeful in its design and has evolved during its various iterations with different groups of teacher candidates. The objective of its use is to find ways to conceive of literacy curricula less as a set of standards or graded course of study that include predetermined lists of knowledge to be obtained and skills to be achieved and more of an ongoing and creative conversation that emerges organically out of the planned, enacted, and received activities in a dynamic classroom. The Critical Conversations Curriculum Chart (CCCC) provides a framework for teacher candidates to structure a curricular unit that spans an entire academic year and prioritizes critical literacy pedagogy (Bender-Slack & Miller-Hargis, 2014; Bender-Slack et al., 2012). It begins with an overarching question, to which the students and teachers will continue to refer throughout the progression and build-up of the unit. The unit is then subdivided in some natural way (by quarters, trimesters, weeks, etc.) with individual discussion questions or prompts for each that, while self-contained, are also recursive, flowing back into the original and principal question. For each of these subdivisions, there is a plan for texts that will be consumed, as well as assignments, activities, or texts to be produced.

As such, the CCCC helps teachers envision and plan for what might be missing. It is effective because it helps teachers consider the types of integrated and transformative curricular conversations that could be initiated, continued, and managed over time. We are looking at not only knowledge acquisition but also the development of critical thinking, the improvement of literate behavior in specific contexts and for explicit purposes, and, most importantly, a call to action for social justice and equity. As Burroughs (1999) indicates, integrated curricular conversations within which "a text is embedded affects how it is understood, experienced, and appreciated by students" (p. 154).

SAMPLE UNIT/LESSON PLAN: CCCC BY ISABEL

In this section, we will provide a sample CCCC designed by a teacher candidate, Isabel, in one of our methods courses and discuss its structure and content (table 2.1). This preservice secondary educator developed a yearlong lesson, subdivided into four quarters, with books, movies, music, and benchmark assignments for each quarter. She designed four overarching questions that echo back to the original question and help focus on the "big picture" of learning in her content area classroom.

This lesson is an exemplar of the CCCC. It begins by providing an overarching question that has the potential of drawing many answers and supporting many conversations. From this question, the teacher can draw upon the knowledge and experience of her students, without leading them directly to specific answers that are required or anticipated. The quarterly questions, which frame smaller units of discussion over the course of the academic year, feed back into the overarching question: "What makes a great society?" For example, students in the first quarter are required to investigate some of the "great ancient societies" and ask themselves, are these the characteristics that make a great society? In the second quarter, the students are asked to bring that question a little "closer to home" by looking at current societies and asking if the structures, ideas, and values these modern societies share help answer the question what makes a society great? The third quarter's query about a "perfect" model will allow them to disrupt a common notion many people share that there is but one "right" way to live and investigate issues of diversity, inclusion, and tolerance. Finally, in the fourth quarter, students are expected to extend the conversations about diversity and inclusion to consider the social justice issues that could be addressed to improve our society and make it a "great society." In this way, the conversations not only build upon one another but are recursive and integrated, allowing for ongoing and meaningful classroom discourse.

In order to fuel the emerging conversations, Isabel has balanced fiction, nonfiction, and alternative texts (such as movie clips and selected lyrics) to support the students' investigation of both the smaller unit questions and the overall unit inquiry. The quarterly units build upon one another but are also recursive in nature. From a unit on understanding the past ("What are

Table 2.1. Isabel's Critical Conversations Curriculum Chart (CCCC)

What Makes a Great Society?

Quarter 1	Quarter 2	Quarter 3	Quarter 4
Overarching question: **What were some of the great ancient societies and how have they influenced the modern world?**	*Overarching question:* **What modern societies are considered great?**	*Overarching question:* **Is there one perfect model for society or can there be more than one right way to organize how we live?**	*Overarching question:* **What social justice issues can we work on to better life in existing societies?**
The students and I will discuss the structure, values, and beliefs of respected ancient societies. We will look for their commonalities and differences; then we will discuss their impact on the modern world.	We will discuss the structure, values, and beliefs in American society, and other countries around the world. We will look for structures, ideas, and values that these societies share.	We will discuss respect for diversity and tolerance for other cultures, as well as the purpose of government and society.	We will discuss how we as individuals can make small changes that have a big impact on the societies that we live in today.
Texts consumed (Fiction): *Anna of Byzantium:* Life in Byzantium from the perspective of an heiress to the throne	**Texts consumed (Fiction):** *America Street:* Collection of multicultural stories about life in America	**Texts consumed (Fiction):** *The Giver:* This book will prompt discussion about the significance of learning from the past and bring about a dialogue around utopia vs. dystopia	**Texts consumed (Fiction):** *Tears of a Tiger:* Deals with issue of teens and drunk driving
Crispin: The Cross of Lead: Life in feudal Europe from the perspective of a peasant	*Teen Ink: What Matters:* Collection of stories, poetry, art, etc., that reveal what is important to teens around the world today	*Lord of the Flies:* This book will prompt a discussion about what happens in the absence of government and what makes us civilized	*On the Fringe:* Deals with bullying *The Secret Story of Sonia Rodriguez:* Deals with illegal immigration and abuse
One Hundred and One African American Read-Aloud Stories: Selected African Tales	**Texts consumed (Nonfiction):** *Teens in China:* Details of life for teens in modern China	**Alternative Texts:** *The Hunger Games* [movie]	*The Breadwinner:* Deals with issue of women's rights in Afghanistan
Selection of Greek Myths: "Perseus and Medusa" and "Pandora's Box"	*If the World Were a Village:* Statistics and information about what life is like around the globe		*A Long Walk to Water:* Deals with life as refugee in Sudan **Alternative texts:** "Where Is the Love?" [song]

Texts consumed (Nonfiction):
China's Buried Kingdoms: From the editors of Time Life

Alternative texts:
Clash of the Titans [movie]

Assignments:
Students will select an ancient society to research. They will write an expository piece and create and present a PowerPoint about their selected society's structure, values, accomplishments, limitations, and contributions to the modern world

Our Century in Pictures for Young People: Photos that depict important moments

Alternative texts:
"We Didn't Start the Fire" [song]

Assignments:
#1 Personal Narrative: Students will write a personal narrative about growing up in America that could be part of their future memoir. They will discuss how their values have been shaped by American society

#2 Collage: Students will create a collage of photos that they think embodies the structure, characteristics, and values of modern American society

Assignments:
#1 Poetry: Students will compose a poem that captures their reaction to one of the texts.

#2 Dialogue: Students will imagine that they are either Katniss or Peeta and have been given the opportunity to speak with President Coriolanus. They will write a dialogue showing how they might try to convince him to end the Hunger Games

#3 Debate: Students will take a pro-con stance on whether or not we should strive to create a perfect society. They will research and write up their points before participating in a formal class debate

Assignments:
#1 Letter Writing Campaign: The class will vote on a social justice issue to advocate, and then write letters to their state senators expressing their concerns and suggesting solutions

#2 Multigenre Project: Students will select a social justice issue that they feel a connection to and create a multigenre project to generate awareness and understanding of the issue

some great ancient societies?") and connecting it to their present experiences
("What modern societies are considered great?"), the teacher continues the
original classroom discourse (looking at life in ancient societies from different social classes) and folds in the same consideration as applied to American
society (how have students' values been shaped by their experience of modern America). Both of these class discourses reflect upon the original question of what makes a great society, even as it moves to the issue of societal
models in quarter 3 (ideas of utopian vs. dystopian societies). What is more,
the entire trajectory of smaller inquiries is intended to lead students to action
to promote social justice by asking what social justice issues might be worked
on to improve life in our existing societies.

It is important to note that the texts chosen are not unusual in many secondary classrooms, even those classrooms that are not designed with the CCCC
in mind. Books like *The Giver* (Lowry, 1993) and *Lord of the Flies* (Golding,
1954) are often taught as English Language Arts canon because they are
traditional texts that show up in many, if not most, required secondary reading. Unfortunately, however, these are often utilized in isolation, with little
context or connection to a larger classroom discourse. Nested here in the
overarching question, their purpose changes, allowing students to critically
engage with questions about what diversity means, what it means to toler-
ate or embrace other cultures, as well as to consider what purposes government has in creating a "civilized" society. Indeed, it even allows students to
consider how we define "civilized," and what it might mean to work toward
creating better lives for ourselves and others. What is more, the overarching
question and CCCC design allows more contemporary literature such as *A
Long Walk to Water* (Park, 2010) and *Teens in China* (Lyons, 2007) and alternative texts like song lyrics seamless integration with more traditional novels.

The activities and assignments, too, are designed to further conversations
and engage students in critical literacy dialogues. Students move between
the personal and the social as they write personal and reflective narratives
that allow them to consider how their values have been shaped by American
society. They are required to consciously engage with the texts they are reading by writing a dialogic exchange with a character in one of stories. They
begin to consider sociopolitical issues as they debate a pro or con stance on
whether or not the perfect society should be an object of attainment, and again
when they select a social justice issue to explore and research. The designer
of this CCCC also allows students to "show what they know" in a variety of
ways: through research and expository writing, through personal narratives
and memoirs, through visual arts such as a collage, through poetry writing,
through the development of research bullet points that support an argument,
through oral debates, through business and personal letter writing, and
through multigenre projects (Romano, 2000) that allow the students to pick

a research topic that interests them and package their ideas together symbolically, using reading, writing, ingenuity, and imagination that is specific to the student as an individual.

This CCCC is a stellar exemplar because it allows students to improve their reading and writing skills as they engage in meaningful and relevant activities related to a broad field of study. The students are required to utilize disciplinary discourse by reading, writing, thinking, talking, and graphically representing as historians do. These historical inquiries and disciplinary traditions are the "knowledge-in-action out of which we construct our realities as we know and perceive them" (Applebee, 1996, pp. 1–2) and allow the teacher and the students to use their classroom conversations to develop skills, engage in critical inquiry, and consider all manner of possibility. As Isabel indicated, "Curriculum originates from our traditions of scholarship in the different disciplines. . . . Its goal is to provide a framework for the body of knowledge and skills that students should acquire . . . throughout their educational skills."

HELPFUL SUGGESTIONS

Upon our writing of this chapter, we offer the following suggestions:

Choose a Relevant Overarching Question

One of the most important (and difficult) aspects of creating a CCCC is to choose an overarching question that is broad enough, yet specific enough, to not only be relevant but also to support many aspects of long-term planning. This is to say that your question should consider not only the content you are teaching and the disciplinary conversations you intend to have but also the students you are teaching and the context in which your classroom exists. Because our students come with a wide range of interests, skills, and lived experiences, the question you choose must be comprehensive enough to include all student voices and allow spaces for every child in your class to engage.

Additionally, because learning does not occur in a vacuum, we must also be sensitive to the fact that the classroom conversations we intend to facilitate will occur in a specific political climate, at a particular school, among parents, faculty, and administration who embrace certain values and ideals. This is not to suggest that any topic is, or should be, "off limits," but it is important to remember that the goal is to provide texts and require activities that allow all children to safely enter the conversation and explore the topic(s) at hand, while concurrently pushing the boundaries. Disrupting the commonplace is a critical component of CCCC planning; finding that key question that will be the impetus for meaningful conversations is really at the heart of it all.

Embrace Varied Texts from Many Sources

For an integrated curriculum to occur, our classroom conversations must be relevant, robust, and recursive. "Old" learning on a topic is revisited while "new" learning is assimilated. While traditional literature may be useful (as we have seen in the CCCC exemplar in this chapter), it is important to remember that texts come in many shapes, sizes, and forms. Photos, newspapers, music lyrics, contemporary literature, sculptures, comic strips, vintage and current cartoons, movie clips, advertisements, guest speakers, social media, TikToks, and even in-person experiences such as field trips can and should be used to interrogate multiple viewpoints, reframe perspectives, and introduce sociopolitical issues in disciplinary domains. The author of our example, Isabel, stated that "critical literacy cuts across the personal and the social and sets students up with a focus and bias toward action for social justice. It requires using different analytical skills to interpret and analyze literature to inform this bias toward action."

Let Your Students Take the Lead as Much and Often as Possible

As we have indicated, classrooms can and should be transformative spaces. While teachers have as a goal the transmission of knowledge and skills, it cannot be our only (or even primary) purpose. If educators are to make a difference in the lives of children they teach, they should inspire students to explore, examine, and contemplate all manner of interpretive possibilities for a future that we, as adults, cannot even begin to conceive. Students should be encouraged to think and read critically so that they can be empowered to change the world in which they exist. This means allowing for conversations that may, for teachers and students alike, be difficult to navigate or manage. Isabel points out that "critical literacy involves valuing students' prior knowledge (their personal and cultural backgrounds) and using it to help them make connections to social issues. They should be able to, with some scaffolding and practice, use their knowledge and understanding to analyze and synthesize data and come up with justice-oriented solutions to problems."

DECONSTRUCTING THE CURRENT SYSTEM OF INSTITUTIONALIZED POWER AND EXISTING IDEOLOGIES OF CURRICULA

By allowing students to engage in difficult conversations and contribute to the trajectory of those conversations as seen in the exemplar above, teachers can *resist context-neutral mindsets* and *transcend cultural conflicts*. Teachers who resist neutral mindsets recognize that teaching and learning do not take place in a vacuum and understand that classrooms are not somehow isolated from the outside world. Teaching and learning are, in fact, reflective of the very milieus in which they exist. Schools and classrooms mirror their surroundings and the individuals involved, including the current political climate, the existing school culture, and the leadership style of the administration, as well as the background and biases of the teacher and parents. These social contexts affect both teaching and learning, not only in the expectations set forth by national, state, and district standards but also in the methods and materials permitted and encouraged. By understanding and acknowledging the ways in which these contexts influence how education works, teachers can empower students to take a closer look at the systems of power that are at work and to confront and resist these.

In a more traditional classroom, for example, it would not be uncommon for a historical unit on great societies to be expected to lead to a foregone conclusion that the American way of life represents the culmination of the "best" that the world and history have to teach us. The CCCC exemplar presented in this chapter challenges the status quo by problematizing the narrative that America is "the greatest country on earth." The CCCC unit developed by Isabel, including all of its readings, activities, and assignments, allows students to use ancient societal models to explore freely and fully the structure, values, and beliefs represented in American society, as well as other countries around the world. This compare-and-contrast methodology encourages students to investigate the purpose of governments, their strengths and their weaknesses, as well as their attentiveness to issues of diversity, inclusion, tolerance, and equity and allows them to draw their own conclusions. It also challenges the students to adopt their own call to action, as the final overarching question requires them to consider how they might make changes that will positively impact their own world and improve the society in which they live.

Racial bias in history textbooks and curriculum is a persistent problem. They perpetuate widespread ignorance and misinformation regarding slavery, omit significant contributions to our society made by persons of color and women, ignore the decimation of Native American culture brought about by the westward expansion, downplay the Japanese internment camps during

World War II, and perpetuate the Eurocentric biases of the past. Utilizing the CCCC allows teachers to obtain, utilize, and integrate materials that offer alternative perspectives; this wide range of resources can encourage students to challenge previously learned information and fuel conversations about issues of diversity and equity. Regardless of their backgrounds, including their families and communities, both students and teacher can engage in critical literacy activities that require them to participate in exploring alternative ways of thinking and being, ultimately mitigating and *transcending cultural conflicts*.

Remember that cultural conflicts can create serious divide and disconnect between teachers and learners and between learners and the content, making teaching and learning difficult. Despite their best efforts, teachers may struggle with the development of cultural competence and the shedding of personal biases and ideologies. Utilizing critical literacy practices through the CCCC allows both educators and students to consciously engage with one another through shared experiences and "real" talk. By considering all manner of possibilities and adopting alternative ways of existing, perceiving, and interacting, students and teachers can improve and deepen their understanding of how our background plays a role in the classroom. Ongoing conversations between and among teachers and students lead to shared power, which, as we have indicated, is critical to the promotion of justice- and equity-based educational processes.

Parting Thought

In your teaching life, what kind of talk do you hear that appears to perpetuate the implicit biases evident in traditional schooling? What type of talk might you encourage with your colleagues to resist and confront this mindset?

Chapter 3

Developing Critical Literacy Lessons through Meaningful Themes

Planning for Emerging Opportunities

Overarching question: How might teachers re-envision traditional thematic units in their classrooms to create meaningful, relevant, critical conversations?

Big Ideas:

- Critical literacy lessons can complement previously designed thematic lessons.
- Elements of critical literacy planning can and should emerge from student interest and inquiry.
- Thematic units can be interdisciplinary.

THEMATIC UNIT STRUCTURE

Thematic units are a way of teaching and learning in which several areas of the curricula are connected within an overarching theme. Thematic instruction assumes that students learn best when they are able to integrate new information holistically across the curriculum and within the context of shared learning experiences and classroom communities. Proponents of thematic pedagogy believe that cohesive units of instruction allow learning to be less fragmented and more natural, permitting students to make connections between and among the many content areas, while concurrently improving literacy skills through authentic reading, writing, speaking, viewing, and listening tasks.

It is important to negate the idea that thematic units *must*, by definition and design, be interdisciplinary, although it allows for multiple opportunities to include other content areas. Whole language classrooms, for example, often focus significant time and attention on thematic reading and writing that may or may not intentionally include instruction in the content areas. The emphasis in a whole language classroom is on reading and writing, tasks are seen as wholes in and of themselves and, as such, learned or "caught" by exposure and experience, rather than "taught" through isolated word analysis, skills and drills, and direct instruction. In whole language classrooms, the focus is on making meaning in reading and writing activities by using high-quality and culturally diverse literature and real-world writing activities. These language events do not happen in a vacuum. Children are encouraged to fully and frequently engage in a wide range of reading experiences, including guided reading groups, teacher read-aloud, and independent reading of complete and cohesive texts. Likewise, writing is an integral part of the meaning-making process where children are encouraged to interpret texts and freely express their understanding by drawing, journaling, and responding to the thematic reading they complete. Even decoding instruction is meaning-centered where phonics is taught contextually through embedded phonics, and the roles of grammar, spelling, capitalization, and punctuation are approached as necessary in diverse social contexts in order to express one's understanding and make meaning clearer. Appealing to students' interests that run across disciplines can add another layer of interest and relevance for student engagement.

To begin, let's consider a common thematic unit for young learners in the primary grades: bears. A traditional thematic unit might focus on the incorporation of content area information around the theme of bears and include activities and experiences that integrate learning, sometimes encouraging learning across disciplines. Reading practice, for example, would likely be connected to written responses; science lessons might naturally connect to artistic endeavors or mathematical equations. In figure 3.1 below, we can see a sample of some of the learning activities that might be part of a traditional thematic unit on bears in the elementary grades.

Each of the content areas could include several activities that overlap learning in another area. For example, a social studies discussion about bear families and community behavior could easily overlap with a more scientific conversation about the process of hibernation. A whole class reading of the literary classic *We're Going on a Bear Hunt* (Rosen, 2009) makes an interesting segue into bear species and their respective habitats. Completing a Venn diagram that compares and contrasts real and imaginary bears is an important prewriting activity to writing a letter to teddy bears that students

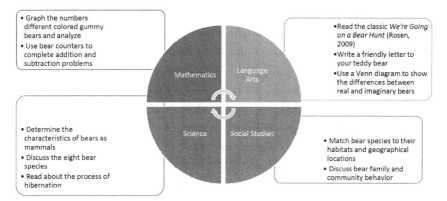

- Graph the numbers different colored gummy bears and analyze
- Use bear counters to complete addition and subtraction problems

Mathematics

Language Arts

- Read the classic *We're Going on a Bear Hunt* (Rosen, 2009)
- Write a friendly letter to your teddy bear
- Use a Venn diagram to show the differences between real and imaginary bears

Science

Social Studies

- Determine the characteristics of bears as mammals
- Discuss the eight bear species
- Read about the process of hibernation

- Match bear species to their habitats and geographical locations
- Discuss bear family and community behavior

Figure 3.1. Thematic Unit on Bears

bring to class. Such learning is more cohesive and natural, allowing children opportunities to use their integrated communication skills of reading, writing, speaking, viewing, listening, and graphically representing in various and authentic ways that center around one particular topic.

Because thematic units are often intended to be interdisciplinary, thematic instruction may require a teams-based approach in older grades where students are not in self-contained classrooms, but they have been a popular way to organize content since the 1960s and 1970s. While the bear unit example above is an innocuous example of thematic planning, themes can also be weighty. Described by some as "the heart of the English curriculum" where "a number of related literary pieces [are examined for] their significance in light of the theme; for example, loneliness, peace, war, and the like" (LGH, Bushart, & Kaplan, 1990), thematic units work well for teachers and students who are able to identify a purpose for their reading and writing, thereby making learning more relevant. They can experience knowledge in a larger context, seeing connections across time, place, disciplines, texts, discourses, and pedagogical activities.

WHAT'S MISSING?

For our purposes, a layer of critical literacy pedagogy, added to more traditional thematic units can provide stimulating opportunities for teachers and learners to investigate concepts in ways that are more consistent with how life is experienced outside of the classroom and, as a result, make learning more relevant to the individuals undertaking the area of study. Themes can be current and student-centered, allowing for the use of the many critical literacy resources and social justice practices suggested by Lewison, Leland,

and Harste (2011). They can incorporate the interests, concerns, needs, and perspectives of the students we are teaching and encourage the critical stance required. What is more, thematic pedagogy closely aligns with the place-based, project-based, and person-focused instruction that can encourage authentic critical dialogue both in and outside of the classroom. Thematic units embrace the same communication processes that are utilized when we disrupt the commonplace, interrogate multiple viewpoints, focus on privilege and power, and take action to promote social justice as we engage in critical literacy practices.

Simply adding a critical literacy perspective will require our young elementary students to adopt a critical stance and might make our earlier traditional thematic unit look more like figure 3.2.

In the thematic unit above, we can see that each of the content areas still overlaps learning occurring in another discipline. For example, graphing the number of bears in math can intersect an analytical conversation about deforestation in science. However, we can also see the ways in which the critical literacy element adds another level of inquiry and knowledge exploration that is both more meaningful and more relevant because it requires students to consciously engage and entertain alternate ways of being. By reading *Believe Me, Goldilocks Rocks!* (Loewen, 2012), which tells the story of Goldilocks and the three bears from Baby Bear's perspective, for example, children disrupt their taken-for-granted understanding of a traditional folk tale and entertain a different perspective of Goldilocks and Baby Bear being "besties" rather than adversaries. The critical literacy Venn diagram activity allows children to articulate their understanding of the similarities and differences between the two texts and begin to consider that all stories have voices that are dominant and those that are silenced, based on who is telling the story and what the author's purpose is in telling the tale. Adding critical pedagogy

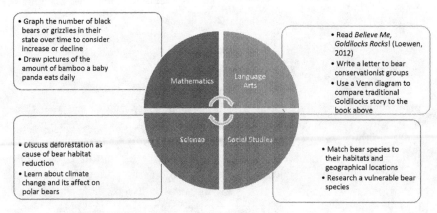

Figure 3.2. Thematic Unit on Bears with Critical Literacy

also provides opportunities for students to investigate timely topics such as climate change and deforestation as human-generated issues that affect some of the most vulnerable among us—like animals, who have no voice and rely on humans to protect them. A follow-up letter to conservationist groups helps students move toward an empowering action, answering the call to become actors in the world to promote justice and equity.

That said, something is still missing from the new critical-literacy-infused thematic unit. Without the big-picture perspective that includes the overarching question, the teacher remains the regulator of learning skills, strategies, and content, and thus, students will not understand an overall purpose or see connections. There is no overarching structure in which the teacher can facilitate the many *knowledge-in-action* conversations that should emerge as these new texts and ideas are embedded in daily planning. With the goal of reducing the teacher's role of dispenser and transmitter of learning skills, content, and strategies and, instead, encouraging respectful, cooperative, and collaborative interaction that is at the heart of critical literacy learning, we must consider once again our unit on bears.

SAMPLE LESSON/UNIT PLAN: INTEGRATED CRITICAL LITERACY THEMATIC INSTRUCTION

Returning yet again to our unit on bears for the early grades, our CCCC unit plan, now designed around critical conversations, might look something like the one shown in table 3.1.

As one can see, the curricular conversations for each week, while supported by the texts that are consumed and the assignments that are required, are linked to the overarching question, "What can bears teach us about organism interdependence?" The unit we designed here, using the CCCC, becomes both inclusive and comprehensive—that is, it is an *integrated* curriculum where the multiple and ongoing conversations from each week are linked to the "theme," to the overarching question, and to one another. The unit (and the discussions within) builds upon itself and creates a curriculum of "independent but interacting experiences" (Applebee, 1996, p. 77) that can both create dialogue and engage the many ideas that will emerge from the students and teacher who are conversing.

The CCCC helps teachers conceive of curriculum as more than just the *what* of learning, but the *how* of learning as well. The overarching question, as well as the weekly questions, are intentionally open-ended so that all children are provided with a space to share whatever knowledge or information they can contribute to the conversation and to explore areas of interest. Some children may know little about live bears and have limited information save

Table 3.1. Bears Critical Conversations Curriculum Chart (CCCC)

What can bears teach us about organism interdependence?

Week 1	Week 2	Week 3	Week 4
Overarching question: **How do bears live and interact with their environment and what does this tell us about them?**	*Overarching question:* **How might changes in the environment affect bears?**	*Overarching question:* **What responsibility do humans have for animals such as bears?**	*Overarching question:* **What can I do to protect and support animals' rights?**
We will explore information about the eight types of bears, the environments in which they live, creatures that share these environments, and discuss their characteristics, habitats, similarities, and differences	We will investigate the environmental changes that occur in the habitats that different bears inhabit and discuss how these changes may affect the quality of the bears' (and other creatures') lives	We will discuss the interactions of humans and animals, the ways in which we share the Earth, and respect for the natural world and the creatures in it.	We will discuss how we, as individuals and groups, can make small changes in our lives that may have a big impact on the quality of life for animals and other living things.
Texts consumed:	**Texts consumed:**	**Texts consumed:**	**Texts consumed:**
National Geographic: Bears: This is a nonfiction text that provides useful background information on bears	*Backyard Bears: Conservation, Habitat, Changes, and the Rise of Urban Wildlife:* This is a nonfiction text that explores how changes in black bear habitats are making them our urban neighbors	*Our Animal Neighbors: Compassion for Every Furry, Slimy, Prickly Creature on Earth:* This is a nonfiction text that introduces children to the importance of treating animals with dignity, care, and respect	*The Magic School Bus and the Climate Challenge:* This fiction text shows children learning about climate change
Tops and Bottoms: This is a fictional retelling of a traditional fairy tale about how Hare tricks Bear into giving up half his crops	**Alternative texts:**	*The Polar Bears' Home:* This fiction text leads children on an adventure as told by a little girl learning about global warming and its effect on polar bears	*A Hot Planet Needs Cool Kids:* This nonfiction text provides the most updated information about global warming and what kids and their parents are doing about it
Believe Me, Goldilocks Rocks! This is a retelling of the popular fairy tale as told from Baby Bear's perspective	*Arctic Tale: National Geographic Documentary [movie]*		
	Easy Science site: https://easyscienceforkids.com		

Alternative texts:

Bears: Disney Documentary [movie]

"Bear Song" [song]

Assignments:

#1 Diorama Project: Research a specific type of bear and create a diorama of the bear in its habitat

#2 Venn Diagram: Compare and contrast real and imaginary bears

#3: T-Chart: Use a T-chart to consider the traditional story of Goldilocks to the Loewen text

Assignments:

#1 Be a Playwright: In a small group, write and act out a play about a bear or bear family and their changing environment

#2 Extending the Diorama: Using the original diorama, add other animals, flora, etc., that could be found in the environment and be prepared to explain how they interact or are connected to your bear

#3 Research Report: Using the Easy Science site, investigate how your bear's environment is changing and write a short report to share orally

Alternative Texts:

Bear (original paintings by Linda Israel) [art prints]

National Geographic site: https://www.natgeokids.com/

Assignments:

#1 Creating Portraits: Using Israel's art as a visual, create a portrait of your specific bear choice from week one

#2 Infographic Posters: Utilize the National Geographic site to learn more about your bear type and, in groups, create a fast fact poster that will inform others about your bear's uniqueness

#3: Critical Quick Lists: Collaborate with a partner and list the things humans can do to protect animals

Alternative texts:

Magic School Bus: Tales Glaciers Tell [animated episode]

Ranger Rick site: https://rangerrick.org

Assignments:

#1: Anticipation of Conservation Activity: With a partner, create a list of conservation activities that kids can do

#2 Conservation Imagination: Write a story about what you have learned from this unit and share it with a younger child

#3: Letter-Writing Campaign: Research a local company or industry that could improve its environmentally conscious behavior and write a persuasive letter

that they have four legs and fur, but all children can express some understanding through the support of the written texts, the alternative texts, and the varied assignments. Rather than reading textbooks about mammal characteristics and being evaluated on them on Friday, the development of this knowledge is contextualized in a broader line of inquiry, making the need for learning it more pressing, motivating, and relevant. Students will use the information for a purpose (other than an assessment), making learning integral and connected, not incidental and separated.

The overarching unit question ("What can bears teach us about organism interdependence?") is intentionally developed and linked to the final call to action to promote social justice. Teachers and students, with the overarching unit question in mind, learn information about animals (including bears), animal habitats, the effect of environmental and human-initiated changes to the environment on animals, consider the ways in which all organisms share the

TEXTBOX 3.1. MOMENT OF REFLECTION: HOW CAN I REINVENT MY CURRENT THEMATIC UNITS?

Planning for a thematic unit that is infused with critical literacy does not mean you must reinvent the wheel. Think about the thematic units you've already planned, assembled, or implemented and answer the following questions:

Does the theme I am choosing provide opportunities for my students to use their funds of knowledge, personal resources, past experiences, or cultural capital to bear on the topic? Is there a way to broaden or modify my theme to include these?

Does the theme I am choosing link to a larger discourse community outside of my classroom? Are scientists or doctors, for example, also talking about this topic in the real world? Are politicians or policy makers currently discussing this topic? If not, how can I modify my theme or what can I include to make the topic timely and relevant to my students' lived experiences?

Does the theme I am choosing allow me to use a wide range of texts, both fiction and nonfiction, traditional and contemporary, print and nonprint? What sources have I used in the past and how can I increase the variety?

Is there a way for the theme I am choosing to lead to action that my students will find meaningful, relevant, and purposeful? What community resources are available to them?

Earth, and finally, consider what individuals can do to improve the quality of life for all of those organisms.

In the final quarter, students are expected to complete three action-oriented assignments: (1) List conservational activities that children can do, (2) write a story about information learned in the unit and share it with a younger child, and (3) engage in a letter-writing campaign that challenges a local company or industry to improve its eco-consciousness or environmental practices. In this way, the lessons in the unit are not only echoing back on one another and integrating new information, but are also "leading somewhere"—that is, encouraging students to make their new knowledge actionable.

HELPFUL SUGGESTIONS

Upon our writing of this chapter, we offer the following suggestions:

Include Alternative Texts

Alternative texts, such as movies, documentaries, animated series, songs, visual art, graphic representations, pictographs, and websites, allow children an opportunity not only to utilize a variety of sources at varying levels of readability but also to engage with the content and one another in a variety of ways. Interactive websites, for example, provide children time to explore specific areas of interest, utilize hyperlinks for deep dives into those areas, and learn vocabulary in meaningful contexts. Images, charts, and other nontext resources are also useful for children with certain cognitive and learning disabilities, allowing them to access information in ways that are more comfortable and captivating. Visual representations are considerate of diverse learners and, when paired with verbal explanations and classroom discourse, help children learn new skills, know what to do, and feel included. These can be especially helpful for children who are learning English as a second language, have limited reading or listening vocabularies, or have other learning impairments.

Embrace Texts with a Wide Range of Readability Levels

In every given classroom, the reading abilities of your individual students can vary greatly. A classroom of third graders, for example, can typically include struggling readers reading at a first-grade level and contain advanced students reading as well as some fifth graders. The representative texts in our unit above include those that are intended to be used by the teacher as a read-aloud or by advanced readers as a resource (e.g., *National Geographic:*

Bears) and those that should be at an independent level for most students in the classroom (e.g., *Tops and Bottoms*). Students provided with texts at varied ability levels will both find opportunities to practice their reading skills at a comfortable level (i.e., their independent level) and also find reason to employ new comprehension strategies for more challenging texts (i.e., their instructional level). The unit developed here also includes varied assignments that provide all children, regardless of their reading and writing ability, to participate, collaborate, and improve their literacy skills

Standards May Matter, but Don't Start There

There is significant evidence that the "standards-based recipe" for teaching and learning often has little if anything to do with how students learn best and usually nothing to do with how teachers teach best (Moore, Jansen, & Hatch, 2003). A focus on starting instructional planning with standards means that many teachers will abandon the type of inquiry-based learning and hands-on activities that we endorse here, opting instead for prescriptive, rote lessons that we find in lessons that begin with the "smallness" of an individual lesson or set of lessons and fail to recognize the big-picture perspective of an entire unit. Furthermore, state-prescribed standards marginalize rather than engage at-risk learners because they only emphasize facts, skills, and definitions and require students to demonstrate mastery in traditional assessments such as multiple-choice tests. Standards-first lesson planning is the antithesis to big-picture curricular development; by definition, it can become a "distraction of the small," the detail-focused learning that counteracts the potential for transformative educational processes and curricular conversations.

Using the CCCC will assist teachers in prioritizing meaningful interactions, relevant texts, evocative talk, and compelling assignments that will increase motivation and the curiosity-based inquiry in which most children naturally engage. As teachers become more confident in organizing learning in this way, they will find that learning outcomes, like the standards, can easily be embedded in unit planning after the curricula have been conceived and organized in a critical-literacy-forward mindset.

Lead Students to Actions That Promote Social Justice

Both the unit introduced in chapter 2 and the bear unit presented here lead to social justice activities. Whether that is a letter-writing campaign to a local company, blogging, video or multimedia storytelling, or creating a list of at-home activities individuals can do on a daily basis, CCCC planning should build to actions that matter. Why else would we engage in actions unless they are moving us toward equity and justice? Students can feel empowered as participatory citizens rather than being mired in feelings of helplessness. Actions fuel hope. The recursive nature of learning and the multiple disciplinary conversations that we manage in a transformative classroom create meaningful experiences that lead students to an understanding of their place as members of a larger community—that is, as citizens of the world.

DECONSTRUCTING THE CURRENT SYSTEM OF INSTITUTIONALIZED POWER AND EXISTING IDEOLOGIES OF CURRICULA

Using the CCCC to reimagine a thematic unit has a bifurcated outcome. On the one hand, redesigning thematic units so that they embrace a recursive conversation and critical literacy stance puts the power of learning and developing relevant curricula in the hands of the teachers and students and prioritizes relevant and timely ideas, needs, and interests. The classroom becomes a place where children are engaged in learning about what interests them rather than memorizing what someone outside the classroom believes is important for them to know. What is more, students are encouraged to explore the content in ways that apply to what they want to know and what they are attempting to do. Moving toward action means that students are setting their own purposes for reading and writing activities, generating greater investment and value in the development of skills that will help them reach those individualized or group goals.

In this way, educators both *denounce deficit mindsets* and *confront the myth of meritocracy*. Allowing students to interactively engage in learning and show what they know in evocative contexts means that all children are able to contribute in pertinent and meaningful ways to the conversations emerging in the classroom. It does not prioritize one type of learning or one type of expressing that learning over another. It negates the notion that there are specific things one must know and exact skills one must have in order to be productive and "successful" in the classroom or in the world, resisting such practices as scripted reading programs and courses of study that provide daily and regimented teaching and learning. It values the knowledge, skills, and dispositions that each child brings to the task and provides opportunities for them to share these for a common purpose and goal.

In a more traditional classroom, it would not be uncommon for instruction to begin with a core standard such as children being required to learn about the characteristics of mammals and habitats and achieving that goal through didactic and direct instruction. This might include textbook reading, memorization, repetitive practice, and eventually some type of assessment such as a test or graded worksheet. Because of this, many children who are disengaged or come to the learning task with limited background knowledge, academic language, or test-taking skills may find it difficult to perform. It is not uncommon for educators not only to have low expectations of students experiencing poverty and students of color, but to also limit the manner in which these students are able to engage in the learning experience and achieve some type of success. As indicated earlier, deficit mindsets often become their own self-fulfilling prophecies, with children rising only to the level set for them. Deficit mindsets permeate classrooms and permit educators to focus on what skills, knowledge, or experiences students are lacking and cannot bring to the classroom, especially when they are compared to the standards applied, either by the graded course of study or by the nature of the pedagogical instruction.

Because critical literacy, as shown here, uses as a starting point the understanding, information, knowledge, and areas of interest the students bring to the classroom conversation, collaboration becomes more natural and organic. Children participate in the ways they are able, given the unique funds of knowledge they bring to any classroom discussion. In the thematic unit represented in the CCCC above, students are able to actively engage with the questions being asked, affording students the opportunity to take responsibility for their own learning as they seek to respond to the questions (questions that do not have only one "correct" answer!). The act of questioning and analyzing allows children to share in the power and trajectory of curricular planning and makes the learning relevant, rather than simply creating a list of facts or information to be committed to memory and then assessed in some superficial, unauthentic manner that is disconnected from the ways in which that knowledge might be useful in the real world.

Furthermore, the use of the CCCC confronts the myth of meritocracy. The curricular conversations that emerge through this design are cooperative and collaborative rather than competitive. Student success, rather than being viewed as the result of individuals' hard work, ability, intelligence, and skill, is now viewed from a collective perspective. *All* students engage in the conversations, contributing questions and responses as their background knowledge, experience, and interest allow. They learn from one another. The integrated curriculum infused with critical literacy requires educators to acknowledge and address the fact that there are many aspects of children's lived experiences that shape both academic and social success. The ongoing and recursive conversations that occur during the unit as it evolves provide openings for the teacher and the children to contribute.

Parting Thought

What individuals in your professional or personal life could provide support for you as you begin to reimagine your lessons and plan for critical pedagogy?

Chapter 4

Interdisciplinary Critical Literacies

Incorporating Critical Literacy Lessons in the Disciplines Using Texts That Matter

Overarching question: How can students engage in critical literacies in the content areas, and how can interdisciplinary teaching and learning be justice oriented?

Big Ideas:

- Disciplinary literacy differs from content area reading in significant ways.
- Disciplinary literacy can encourage and motivate struggling readers, especially in adolescence, when reading becomes more content heavy and sophisticated.
- Interdisciplinary teaching and learning can deepen content learning and provide a purpose for the development of literacy skills and strategies.

INTERDISCIPLINARITY

Interdisciplinary teaching and learning are natural; therefore, engaging in critical literacy events in and across disciplines is important and valuable for both instructional and motivational purposes. How one reads, writes, thinks, values, views, speaks, listens, and visually represents is particular to each discipline. These multiple perspectives enrich and deepen student learning, helping students see connections that might have remained hidden to them with a traditional curriculum that is often disconnected, disjointed, and taught

43

in ways that keep content separate and fail to highlight overlap and continuity between and among subject matters.

An interdisciplinary approach typically involves a focus on connecting disciplines with current, everyday themes and ideas. This approach emphasizes process and meaning rather than product and content by combining contents, theories, methodologies, and perspectives from two or more disciplines.

It is not always possible or even helpful to dissolve the boundaries between the conventional disciplines; organizing teaching and learning around the construction of meaning in the context of real-world problems or themes often requires that we cross disciplinary or content boundaries. As you plan for interdisciplinarity, it is important that you consider power dynamics. There are power dynamics to attend to when incorporating multiple disciplines because content area teachers who are planning and instructing have varied but imbalanced strengths and interests.

CONTENT AREA LITERACY VERSUS DISCIPLINARY LITERACIES

Championed since the 1920s by the reading community, content area reading began with an emphasis on all teachers with the common slogan: *All teachers are teachers of reading*. And in some respect, that was accurate, but in many ways, it oversimplified the notion that all teachers teach reading and can do so in the same way and for the same purposes. At that time, teachers received cross-disciplinary training in how to teach reading using content area instructional materials and were encouraged to consider ways to integrate some form of reading comprehension skill or strategy into their content area classrooms.

Content area reading and disciplinary literacy, however, differ by source, the nature of skills, the instructional focus, the impact on students, the types of texts used, and the way graphics were taught. Consider table 4.1 below.

Table 4.1. Content Area Reading versus Disciplinary Literacy

	Content Area Reading	Disciplinary Literacy
Source	Reading experts since the 1920s	Wider range of experts since the 1990s
Nature of skills	Generalizable	Specialized
Focus	Use of reading and writing to study/learn information	How literacy is used to make meaning within a discipline
Students	Remedial	Whole distribution
Texts	Often encourages use of literary text	Only focuses on disciplinary text
Graphics	Ignored or taught generally	Specific to the discipline

The important idea is that there is an increasing specialization of literacy in each content area that significantly impacts readers as their content courses use texts and standards that are increasingly specialized and specific to each discipline. That is to say that every discipline not only uses content-specific vocabulary but also includes specific text formats, nonfiction text structures, and graphics. The problem with content area reading, then, is that literacy is not as generalizable as once thought; disciplinary literacy highlights the idea that some practices make no sense in certain disciplines, and its strategies have been more helpful to struggling readers.

DISCOURSE THEORY

From a sociocultural perspective, literacy is not situated in the abilities of an individual but rather literacy is positioned in society where it interrelates with the workings of power (Gee, 1990). Consequently, we find Discourse Theory to be a helpful theoretical lens through which to understand disciplinary literacies.

Gee defines Discourse (with a capital D) as ways of being in the world, specifically forms of life that integrate words, acts, values, beliefs, attitudes, and social identities with the more concrete gestures, glances, body positions, and clothes. A primary Discourse, which is learned in the home, constitutes our first identity. The primary Discourse also serves as a framework for acquiring and learning future Discourses. Moreover, a secondary Discourse is learned and acquired outside the home in other social settings, in this case, the acquisition of a disciplinary Discourse. Acquiring or learning a secondary discourse extends our use of not just language but also one's values and beliefs. For this reason, we learn to think, act, and speak like a mathematician/historian/scientist.

One becomes literate when one has mastered a secondary Discourse. Because this lens is sociocultural, instruction must occur inside of or within the Discourse. For example, to master a scientific Discourse, one would need to spend time interacting with scientists in a laboratory doing what scientists do and engaging the way scientists engage. In order to master a secondary Discourse or to becoming "literate" in that discipline, it is not enough to simply read about a Discourse, in this case reading lab notebooks and science articles. Consequently, since one has to be positioned inside the Discourse, learning from others who already have accessed that Discourse (for example, one cannot just read about biology and acquire or learn the Discourse but must be working with other biologists doing what they do), the Discourses and their associated literacies are linked to power. If you cannot enter the biologist's lab and work with other biologists to see what they do, how they think, and what they value, you will not acquire that Discourse.

Before attempting to engage in interdisciplinary teaching, practice identifying a disciplinary Discourse with table 4.2, using the history example as a template.

It is often a challenge to articulate what our disciplinary Discourses involve, especially if we are so embedded in them. Ask colleagues in your discipline to help tease out these ideas, and then share them with students. Due to the increased specialization of literacy in each content area for adolescents, teachers can help students engage with content courses' texts and standards that are increasingly specialized and specific to each discipline.

Table 4.2. Disciplinary Discourse Identification

	History (Example)	Your Discipline Here
How do we read? For what purpose are we reading?	History is the study of change. Historians read and write to understand the past and why there is change throughout history and why thoughts and behaviors were pervasive in certain societies	
What kinds of texts do we write? What do we use to do that?	Historians write historical analysis. Historians use primary source documents (photograph papers, personal correspondence, books, etc.) and secondary source documents	
Where and when do we speak, using this Disciplinary Discourse? Where do the experts speak?	Historians speak in their own Discourse communities with articles, journals, conference presentations, documentaries, and through publications	
What are we viewing?	Historians view maps, globes, period photographs, films, primary and secondary source documents, historical writings, and statistics to draw conclusions	
What visual representations are we creating?	Historians create charts, graphs, slides, timelines, period photographs, films, documentaries, and exhibits	
What do we value?	Historians value truth and documentation of what actually occurred, multiple perspectives	
What are our patterns of thinking?	Historians find reliable resources, analyze for thought and behavior patterns, and create timelines, using cause and effect and chronology	

ADOLESCENT LITERACY

With a continued historical focus on emergent and early childhood literacy, adolescent literacy has often been neglected. This was problematic in the initial instructional response because its implementation of adolescent literacy was that it was frequently taught as an extension of primary grade literacy—that is, simply adding reading to the content area curricula and language arts instruction. Too often this meant developing instruction with a reading textbook, monitoring learning outcomes with DIBELS-style assessments, and/or supervision and support from elementary reading coaches or specialists.

Due to the dense and content-specific texts adolescents are assigned in high school, it is no wonder we have what has been termed the *quiet crisis* with so many adolescents struggling with these texts and ultimately dropping out of school. It is difficult to understand how students can do well in grade school, but then falter in high school. However, if we consider the fact that that reading ability is not a general skill but a specific skill *for* specific subjects *to* specific audiences *with* specific background knowledge, it is not as difficult to see how students may struggle. Quite simply, much of what we learn about a subject in schools is how to read and write the texts of a subject—and these "ways of knowing" texts are perhaps more important than the content itself—the ways of knowing can and should be lifelong skills that help us understand research that is cited (e.g., drinking milk helps you lose weight) or a cause-and-effect political argument (e.g., impact of climate change).

The lesson for teachers is that the link between interdisciplinary and adolescent literacy is that the more specialized the disciplinary discourses, the more intentional and explicit teachers must be by defining and articulating their disciplinary Discourse.

Moments of crisis and rupture can be used to focus on curriculum integration that dissolves the boundaries between conventional disciplines. Pandemics, wars, climate change, and other sociopolitical and sociocultural events show us that every issue is constructed by and constructs disciplinary knowledge. Depending on a teacher's background, engaging in critical literacy across disciplines could include two or more disciplines, providing a multidisciplinary approach: The same topic can, and often should, be studied from the viewpoint of more than one discipline.

Interdisciplinary teaching at the deepest level refers to the concept of learning a single subject from multiple perspectives. Learning across disciplines has been known to boost learning outcomes and excitement around learning; interdisciplinary learning allows students to think critically, identify their own prejudices, accept the unknown, and critically analyze ethical quandaries. Interdisciplinary learning also enables students to view content from different disciplines, synthesize information surrounding a topic, and, ultimately, offer a more complete and holistic conception of an issue, like climate change, immigration, racial injustice, and poverty. Interdisciplinary teaching goes beyond multidisciplinary or cross-disciplinary teaching, which only requires the consideration of different perspectives, and requires collaboration between multiple educators to properly implement. If this sounds complicated, it should. It is intricate and difficult.

WHAT'S MISSING?

So, let's complicate it further with the notion of intersectionality, which is about how oppressions (race, class, gender, etc.) intersect (Crenshaw, 1989). Historically responsive literacy practices, too, allow for students to pursue culturally relevant literacy activities that draw upon and respond to students' histories, identities, and literacies (Muhammad, 2020). In utilizing them, teachers are able to consider how their pedagogy will help their students learn something about themselves and others, while building literacy skills and content knowledge and concurrently engaging students' consideration of power and equity.

Muhammad (2020) shares the lessons learned from Black literary societies that relate to the instructional and curricular work we are promoting here (textbox 4.1).

As we have indicated in previous chapters, Milner delineates five interconnected areas that are critical in helping educators shed light on and bridge opportunity gaps for the purpose of promoting equity in education: (1) the rejection of colorblindness; (2) the development of skills to understand, work through, and transcend cultural conflicts; (3) overcoming the myth of meritocracy; (4) the denunciation of deficit mindsets; and (5) the resistance of context-neutral mindsets and practices.

In conjunction and in support of Milner's ideas for promoting equity, the Social Justice Standards from Learning for Justice (previously Teaching Tolerance) are a set of anchor standards and age-appropriate learning outcomes divided into four domains—identity, diversity, justice, and action (IDJA). The standards provide a common language and organizational structure: Teachers can use them to guide curriculum development, and administrators can use them to make schools more just, equitable, and open. The standards are leveled for every stage of K–12 education and include school-based scenarios to show what antibias attitudes and behavior may look like in the classroom (see textbox 4.2). Teaching about IDJA allows educators to engage in a range of antibias, multicultural, and social justice issues.

TEXTBOX 4.1. BLACK LITERARY SOCIETY LESSONS

1. Literacy learning encompassed cognition (reading and writing skills) as well as social and cultural practices (learning about identity and equity).
2. Literacy was the foundation and was central to all disciplinary learning.
3. Literacy learning involved print and oral literacy, and these were developed simultaneously.
4. Literacy instruction was responsive to the social events and people of the time.
5. Literacy was tied to joy, love, and aesthetic fulfillment.
6. Learners of different literacies and experiences came together to learn from one another—using each other's ways of knowing as resources for new learning.
7. Literacy learning was highly collaborative, and a shared learning space was created.
8. Literacy learning involved reading and writing diverse text genres and authorship.
9. Literacy learning also focused on how to reclaim the power of authority in language through critical literacy.
10. Identity and intellectual development were cultivated alongside literacy learning (pp. 32–35).

We believe all of these have a place in critical interdisciplinary instructional planning. What of the above lessons can you incorporate into your planning? Highlight them and use them as instructional goals.

SAMPLE CCCCS

In order to understand what this interdisciplinary approach might look like in the overall vision of the school year, the following two examples, created by teacher candidates during their program, show the types of questions and literacy events that accompany these curricular conversations. Working across the boundaries of social studies and ELA, teacher candidate Michelle Kohler envisioned and designed a CCCC (table 4.3) for students to answer the overarching question: *How does the government influence our lives and affect our choices?*

TEXTBOX 4.2. IDJA ANCHOR STANDARDS

Identity

1. Students will develop positive social identities based on their membership in multiple groups in society.
2. Students will develop language and historical and cultural knowledge that affirm and accurately describe their membership in multiple identity groups.
3. Students will recognize that people's multiple identities interact and create unique and complex individuals.
4. Students will express pride, confidence, and healthy self-esteem without denying the value and dignity of other people.
5. Students will recognize traits of the dominant culture, their home culture, and other cultures and understand how they negotiate their own identity in multiple spaces.

Diversity

6. Students will express comfort with people who are both similar to and different from them and engage respectfully with all people.
7. Students will develop language and knowledge to accurately and respectfully describe how people (including themselves) are both similar to and different from each other and others in their identity groups.
8. Students will respectfully express curiosity about the history and lived experiences of others and will exchange ideas and beliefs in an open-minded way.
9. Students will respond to diversity by building empathy, respect, understanding, and connection.
10. Students will examine diversity in social, cultural, political, and historical contexts rather than in ways that are superficial or oversimplified.

Justice

11. Students will recognize stereotypes and relate to people as individuals rather than representatives of groups.
12. Students will recognize unfairness on the individual level (e.g., biased speech) and injustice at the institutional or systemic level (e.g., discrimination).

13. Students will analyze the harmful impact of bias and injustice on the world, historically and today.
14. Students will recognize that power and privilege influence relationships on interpersonal, intergroup and institutional levels and consider how they have been affected by those dynamics.
15. Students will identify figures, groups, events, and a variety of strategies and philosophies relevant to the history of social justice around the world.

Action

16. Students will express empathy when people are excluded or mistreated because of their identities and concern when they themselves experience bias.
17. Students will recognize their own responsibility to stand up to exclusion, prejudice, and injustice.
18. Students will speak up with courage and respect when they or someone else has been hurt or wronged by bias.
19. Students will make principled decisions about when and how to take a stand against bias and injustice in their everyday lives and will do so despite negative peer or group pressure.
20. Students will plan and carry out collective action against bias and injustice in the world and will evaluate what strategies are most effective.

This exemplary CCCC clearly shows direction toward social justice thought and action. From the initial question of how governmental control and decision-making affect our daily lives to the final question of how we can be participatory members of the governmental process, the varied texts support a critical engagement across historical, political, and literacy lines. This teacher candidate utilizes a wide range of production-oriented (poetry, drama, playwrighting, letter and journal writing) as well as oral production such as debating and simulation to explore the concepts in meaningful and disciplinary-specific ways. This provides ample opportunities for students to engage in the "talk" of the specific content areas, while concurrently adopting a critical lens on the topic at hand.

Teacher candidate Olivia Masuck-Lane designed the following CCCC (table 4.4), using both ELA and science. Her overarching question is: *Who is responsible for our Earth?*

Table 4.3. Michelle Kohler's CCCC

How much effect does the government have on our daily lives?	What happens when the government has too much control?	What would take place in a world with no governing power?	How can you participate in government?
During this quarter, students will be introduced to different aspects that the government controls.	For this quarter, there will be a focus upon government having too much power and overcontrolling the lives of their people.	This section deals with the opposite situation from the previous quarter, where we focus upon what may take place if a government was not in place.	The students will spend this final quarter looking into different ways that they can get involved and help get their voices heard.
Books:	**Book:**	**Book:**	**Books:**
1. *Separate Is Never Equal: Sylvia Mendez and Her Family's Fight for Desegregation,* Duncan Tonatiuh—Sylvia is a Hispanic American who speaks perfect English and was born in America but is refused entrance to a "Whites only" school. Her parents organize the Hispanic community and file a lawsuit in federal court, which brings an end to segregated education in California.	1. *The Giver,* Lois Lowry—Jonas lives in a community where the government has implemented "Sameness." But Jonas is chosen to be given memory and struggles with everything he is learning about the world.	1. *The Girl Who Owned a City,* O. T. Nelson—Everyone over the age of 12 has been killed by a virus. The children left behind begin to form a type of government to help ensure their safety and well-being.	1. *We the Kids: The Preamble to the Constitution of the United States*—This picture book breaks down the Preamble in an easy to read way with drawings that aid in understanding.
	Alternative Materials:	**Alternative Materials:**	a. After reading this book, the teacher will facilitate a discussion regarding why the Preamble is important to us today.
2. *Weedflower,* Cynthia Kadohata—After Pearl Harbor a Japanese American girl and her family is sent to an internment camp because Americans start to believe all Japanese people are spies for the emperor.	1. I Civics, Executive Command Game—Try to further the agenda of your chosen area while dealing with different challenges and trying to keep the public happy.

a. Discussion will follow regarding how the government can choose to focus on their own agenda rather than the agenda the nation wants. https://www.icivics.org/games/executive_command | 1. Video clip—"A Day without Government"—In this video, a day without having any type of government regulations is shown. This video will be shown after the debates are over to help pull together ideas regarding what would happen with no government. Discussion would follow about the clip and how it relates to the novel and the debates. https://www.youtube.com/watch?v=9nXib6tLrHc | 2. *Malala, a Brave Girl from Pakistan/Iqbal, a Brave Boy from Pakistan: Two Stories of Bravery,* Jeanette Winter—This is the stories of two Pakistani children who stood up for the rights of freedom and education. |

Short Article:

1. "Government Is Good—A Day in Your Life," Amy Douglas—This article is a timeline throughout the day of everything one encounters that is regulated by the government. http://governmentisgood.com/articles.php?aid=1&print=1

Activity:

1. Play writing—Students will choose one of the books being read this quarter and research the government's point of view/actions in the situation. The students will then write a play that is based off of the chosen book, but instead is based around the government's point of view/actions of the situation.

2. Poetry book—Students will write two pieces of poetry based upon the emotions felt by the main characters in the novels. The students will follow the writing process and then peer edit each other's pieces.

Activities:

1. Ceremony of 12 simulation—Students will be assigned different jobs just like characters in *The Giver* were. They will be given information describing the job assigned. Discussion will follow regarding whether students think this is a form of government control and why a government would want to do this.

2. Letter writing—Students will need to either write a letter asking for a job change or thanking the government for their assigned job that they were given during the ceremony of 12.

3. Writing assignment—The president has ordered that anyone under the age of 18 is no longer allowed to use any type of electronics at any time. The students will be asked to write about how they feel regarding the decision and what they would do if they do/do not agree with it.

Activities:

1. Tug of war—The question "would the world stay the same or be different if there was no governing power?" will be introduced to students. A yes and a no side will be displayed on the front board. Students will be given Post-It notes and write "tugs" (reasons/examples why they support one side) and put the Post-It on the side it is supporting.

2. Debate—Students will be divided into groups and asked to choose one of the aspects discussed during tug of war. They will research this topic and put together a debate that will be argued in front of the class.

3. Journal Reflections—After each debate, the students will write a journal reflection discussing which side they agree with most and why.

Alternative Materials:

1. Video clip—"How to Change the World (a Work in Progress)" https://youtu.be/4z7gDsSKUmU

2. Video clip—"Emma Gonzalez: 'Fight for Your Lives Before It's Someone Else's Job'" https://youtu.be/Dz6YarZ5upE

Activity:

1. Make a difference!—Each student will choose an area in their community that they feel needs improvement. They will research different approaches and choose the best idea. Then create a realistic plan that the child can do to help fix this problem. An emphasis needs to be made by the teacher that these plans must be things that are actually doable by people their age.

2. Once finished, students will publish their poems, and the teacher will create a classroom poetry book.
3. Research paper—After reading the short article, students would choose two or three of the topics discussed that they do not know anything about. Students will spend time researching the areas chosen and then write a paper discussing each area, while also comparing and contrasting each.
4. Individual novel study—students will choose one of the following books:
   a. *A Thunderous Whisper*, Christina Diaz Gonzalez—Ani befriends Mathis, whose father is a part of a spy network. Soon, Ani becomes a part of this network, but then her town is destroyed by Nazi bombers and she loses everything.
   b. *Number the Stars*, Lois Lowry—The Rosen's are a Jewish family living in Denmark during WWII. The story is based around their struggles and plans to escape the war.
   c. *Milkweed*, Jerry Spinelli—This story is about a Jewish Polish orphan who lives on the streets. One day, trains come to the ghetto and take all the children away to concentration camps. The story revolves around the horrors experienced within these camps.

2. Present it!—The students will create a presentation regarding their plan, which will be given to the other students in the class. The aim of this is to sway the class to vote for your plan.
3. Do it!—After the presentations, the students will vote for the plan that they like most. The voting process will be similar to how adults vote. The winning plan will be completed by the class. Groups of students will be assigned different aspects of the plan. If the group feels their part of the plan should be changed, they must put together their argument and present it to the rest of the class to vote on.

While reading their books, students will keep a reflection journal and record their thoughts on what is being read. These thoughts will be discussed on a regular basis with the whole class. After finishing the book, the students will create a PowerPoint presentation about the main character and how the government controlled their lives, how this made the character feel and how the book would have been different if the government controls were not there/were not as strong.

4. Presentation—After completing the improvement plan, each group will create a 1-minute description describing/showing what they were in charge of. The teacher will record the students talking about their part of the plan and then create a video explaining the process the students took to fix this issue/problem.

Table 4.4. Olivia Masuck-Lane's CCCC

First Quarter	Second Quarter	Third Quarter	Fourth Quarter
What do you know about deforestation? This quarter, students will explore both local and distant deforestation from their neighborhoods to the Amazon rain forest.	**Why do we question climate change?** For the second quarter, students will learn about the reality of climate change and why people continue to question its existence.	**What kind of impact can I make locally?** In quarter three, students will start locally by learning about things they can do in their own communities to help our planet.	**How can we help globally?** To wrap up the year, students will look back at all the work they've done for their local community and expand their advocacy to a global scale.
Students will read: Adrian Forsyth, *How Monkeys Make Chocolate: Foods and Medicines from the Rainforest* Students will learn about the plants, animals and people of the rain forest and their web of interdependence. (*Global Deforestation*)	**Students will read:** Jan Thornhill, *The Tragic Tale of the Great Auk* Students will learn about a species of flightless birds known as Auks that went extinct due to climate change. **Activity:** Students will look at a series of climate change ads and political cartoons regarding climate change. The class will discuss how climate change can affect their neighborhood, circling back to their argumentative presentations in Q1 for evidence and support.	**Students will read:** Carol Liu, *Arlene the Rebel Queen* Arlene and her friends face opposition when she attempts to diminish her school's carbon footprint. Students will explore how Arlene can be an advocate for change. **Activity:** After taking a field trip to Rumpke Recycling Center, students will discuss how recycling can positively impact our planet, can possibly hinder climate change (Q2), as well as help out their local community (Q1). Students will be asked to write up a proposal for a school-wide recycling program (writing). The best proposal will be put into action at school!	**Students will read:** Free choice! Students will pick an environmental issue they are passionate about and find a book that accompanies that topic. Teacher must approve topic and book. **Activity:** Students will create an environmental advocacy journal which briefly outlines deforestation in their local community with their stance (good/bad) (Q1), a reflection or climate change (Q2), and their recycling proposal (C3). In addition to this, students will research their environmental topic of choice by reading their book with a critical eye and analyzing propaganda that speaks against their movement.
Carl Hiassen, *HOOT* An ecological mystery novel which follows Roy, a new kid at school who sets out to save some burrowing owls from developers. (*Local Deforestation*)			

Activity: Find examples of deforestation in your neighborhood, take photos, and create an argumentative presentation (visually representing) on why this deforestation is good or bad for the existing environment.

Students will then be split into groups of four and randomly assigned a political stance on climate change. Students will be asked to perform a debate (speaking) and present both sides. Class will discuss the differing views together.

Students will present their findings and an action plan to the entire school. (Student with the best action plan will choose a nonprofit organization related to their environmental issue and donate all proceeds that come from Miss Masuck's Environmental Advocacy Bake Sale to that organization.)

Olivia clearly moves in the direction of action, both at a local and global level. She seamlessly integrates science concepts such as deforestation with carefully chosen pieces of literature. She asks students to challenge a politically charged question regarding climate change and asks them to investigate opposing arguments with a critical lens, allowing them opportunities to engage in the "real" talk of scientific debate. This teacher candidate also utilizes fieldwork (a class trip to a landfill and a photo journal of local deforestation), social justice planning (a recycling program), and extension activities (analyzing propaganda and independent research) to explore the concept of environmental advocacy through an interdisciplinary process.

HELPFUL SUGGESTIONS

Upon our writing of this chapter, and the reflection it inspired, we offer the following suggestions:

Do Critical Literacy Work That Crosses Disciplines, Helping You to Think Holistically and Prevent the Distraction of the Small

Know your disciplinary Discourse, your content, and know your students so that you can plan instruction accordingly. Do not force connections; there is no need because they already exist in the context of the world which we share. Do not get stuck in standards because those change and student learning is not dependent on standards. In fact, standards are a construction, not a representation. Take your cue not from the curriculum as it is set; take your cue from how connections exist in the real world.

Recognize How the Way We Have Historically Taught Our Disciplines May Limit Us

For example, history has been a story told by victors, English Language Arts is founded on the canon (dead, White male authors), and science is dependent on static and shifting paradigms. Those histories and traditions will impact—and may limit—interdisciplinary work. Thinking outside of these boxes requires us to be creative and to use our "social imagination," which is our capacity to devise visions of what could be and should be to improve things in our deficient society and schools (Greene, 1995).

Plan to Disrupt the Commonplace

With regard to critical literacies, you can only disrupt the commonplace if you really know your content, its history, and its current conversations across the field. In order to include multiple perspectives, search for diverse texts, going global whenever possible, to give full range to voices and peoples and places. This means that your focus should be on staying abreast of ongoing conversations in your discipline and addressing the sociopolitical aspects of your disciplinary discourse by choosing relevant and timely content in every area. Take action in ways that are relevant, give voice to the marginalized, disrupt power structures, and focus on power because democracy is clearly unfinished, perhaps more so in our schools where communities continue to engage in book banning and the policing of curricula.

DECONSTRUCTING THE CURRENT SYSTEM OF INSTITUTIONALIZED POWER AND EXISTING IDEOLOGIES OF CURRICULA

It is difficult to imagine a time when curricula were not separated into distinct disciplines and school days not segmented into structured blocks of time. If that is, indeed, difficult to imagine, then how do we envision something better? For example, Indigenous tribes in the United States had their own educational systems where each family member played a role, and knowledge was transferred from tribal elders to the young people. History, culture, and spiritual beliefs were passed on through oral tradition and practical experiences in a natural, intentional, and cooperative learning environment.

Literacy campaigns, another example of interdisciplinary learning and teaching, have occurred around the globe for more than four hundred years. Set within a specific time frame, they have typically been related to efforts of centralizing authorities to establish a moral or political consensus and associated with major transformations in social structures and belief systems, with a profound triggering event. Campaigns embraced the formation of a new type of person in a qualitatively different society; literacy was not a goal but a vehicle for a larger process. Justice-oriented critical literacy work, whether it includes history, politics, economics, or religion, can transform lives, giving people a voice in their own communities.

There is a popular hashtag, #curriculumsowhite, that has been used by teachers, parents, and students to address the lack of diversity in a lot of school curricula. Consequently, engaging in an antiracist analysis of the curriculum in every content area is critical work for teachers and students alike. We disrupt the commonplace when we question why content is valuable, a text is worthy of reading, or a concept is worthy of study. "So White" curriculum continues to be perpetuated in the US, often under the guise of "that's what we've always done," because schools, with their institutionalized power, are slow to change. Teachers have the power to make meaningful changes based on critical analyses of curricular content, standards, and disciplinary texts in light of the equity and justice we would like to see in schools today.

Our work over the last twenty years, teaching critical literacy and curricula to teachers of middle school students, has helped to work in cross-disciplinary ways. In our state, students majoring in middle childhood choose two areas of concentration, or two disciplines. If taught with an interdisciplinary perspective, this helps them learn and teach with an interdisciplinary focus. But what is needed are teachers who are willing contributors and good at collaborating with other colleagues. Engaging with critical literacies, knowing their disciplinary Discourses, and reaching across those differences as they promote equity and justice will engage students and transform schools into places of hope where all students can thrive.

Parting Thought

If, as Freire suggested, education began with critical dialogue, how could schools be different?

Chapter 5

International Classrooms

Global Networks and Leading with Hope

Overarching question: How will I model being a global citizen, building a global network, and leading with hope?

Big Ideas:

- I must be intentional when learning more about the world.
- Intercultural competence is the ability to interact with people from different cultures, which takes time, patience, the ability to listen and observe, and, quite frankly, the desire.
- The biggest challenges of our time are interconnected, so classrooms should reflect and contribute to that.

GLOBAL AWARENESS AND KNOWLEDGE

When we think of global awareness and knowledge, we are reminded of the old adage—You don't know what you don't know. We also can find ourselves feeling very overwhelmed because, truthfully, we will never know all there is to know about the variety of cultures, languages, and communities around the world. But with an eye always toward a transformative and hopeful future, we encourage, embolden, and implore you: Do not let uncertainty or feelings of futility lead to paralysis, resistance, or surrender!

Love (2020) states that teachers must choose "to engage in the struggle for educational justice knowing that you have the ability and human right to refuse oppression and refuse to oppress others, mainly your students" (p. 11). Turning our attention to the world as we struggle for educational justice will take time and effort. Even when we think we are getting a broader, global perspective, we might subsequently discover that we were mistaken or the view was limited. Much of our global knowledge has been acquired and told (and often still is) by the colonizers, so it is important to use a critical lens when engaging with texts. Consequently, a recognition of power dynamics is critical to understanding historical and current international connections. For example, mission trips are often an echo of the colonizer-colonized relationships, prompting questions like: Who has the power in this situation? Who caused this situation? Whose voices are being heard? Whose needs are being met? To be honest, although some may assert that mission trips do a lot of good, we would assert that, quite often, they have been used as a way for White colonizers to feel better about themselves and their White privilege in the short term.

Once, on a plane to Nicaragua, I (Laney) was sitting next to a woman who was part of the mission trip. She was part of a group of fifteen to twenty people, all wearing matching neon-green t-shirts with the words written in English. I find mission trip t-shirts problematic for a number of reasons, but her group's, quite frankly, stopped me in my tracks. It said, *We are here to save!* Knowing Nicaraguans fairly well, I thought, Who needs to be saved? My Nica friends are lovely, their beliefs spiritual, and their families united.

So I decided to strike up a conversation with the woman next to me who described a camp that her church had for children in a rural area and that they had built a swimming pool and camp area to host the neighborhood children. They taught the children to swim and allowed them time to play in the water. After describing a typical camp day, she mentioned that not all the area children were allowed to attend and use the pool. Feeling extremely curious, I asked, "How do you decide who gets to go swimming and who doesn't?"

"Well, the church keeps track of the number of Sundays they attend church service, and if they go most of the time, they get to swim." This carrot-and-stick or coercion was the same thing that was happening in the barrio of friends in Nicaragua, where a church would make the beans and rice but were not willing to serve it to the people unless they first attended a religious gathering.

During some diversity training, a colleague mentioned that, through a mission trip when he was younger, he once wore a shirt that said, *Bringing God to the ghetto!* He said that it wasn't until that discussion that he recognized that shirt message as being problematic (the assumption that God was not already in that neighborhood). We believe that once students can identify their role in the timeline of colonialization and that they play a role in current inequities, they can begin to act responsibly.

Perhaps as evolving global citizens, we must first construct the idea of global citizenship as a radical de-centering. As two US citizens, we recognize

TEXTBOX 5.1. INTERCULTURAL JOURNAL

Global Awareness Idea

Keep an intercultural journal where you can reflect on and consider intercultural differences and commonalities that you observe and/or negotiate in your daily interactions with people from other cultural groups. This might include your attitudes, values, and behaviors during these intercultural exchanges. The following questions may help you unpack this:

What worked or went well?
Where did you feel tension or resistance?
What can you do better the next time?

that de-centering ourselves in work and in life is difficult—and even more so when traveling outside the US. We should explore what radical de-centering might look like inside and outside of schools, but, of course, this would have to be done in collaboration with people from across the globe. This endeavor is both personal and professional for teachers.

INTERCULTURAL COMPETENCE

Developing the abilities to interact with people from different cultures depends first on a person's ability to recognize their own cultural norms (attitudes, values, and behaviors), and then on their willingness and abilities to understand others' cultural norms. Therefore, this takes time, patience, the ability to listen and observe, and, quite frankly, the desire.

Both teachers and students can work at meeting global competencies—and in various similar ways. The following four global competencies by the Asia Society (Mansilla & Jackson, 2011) demonstrate the types of students we hope to cultivate in global classrooms:

1. Students investigate the world beyond their immediate environment, framing significant problems and conducting well-crafted and age-appropriate research.
2. Students recognize perspectives, others' and their own, articulating and explaining such perspectives thoughtfully and respectfully.
3. Students communicate ideas effectively with diverse audiences, bridging geographic, linguistic, ideological, and cultural barriers.

4. Students take action to improve conditions, viewing themselves as players in the world and participating reflectively.

These four competencies are broad and succinct, while attending to the behavioral, cognitive, and social-emotional domains, which is why they support teacher growth as well.

Viewed along a continuum, global competence is something individuals move along, most never reaching true global competence. Still, these competencies are a helpful guide for teachers wanting to internationalize their classrooms and for both teachers and students who want to develop globally competent dispositions, skills, and strategies.

Using Applebee's notion of knowledge-in-action rather than knowledge-out-of-context, intercultural competencies will only be developed using the former, knowledge-in-action. In classrooms, it is important to note that intercultural competence is not just *learning about* the other but rather *learning in collaboration with* others. Being immersed in other cultures for any period of time is the best way to develop your intercultural competencies. That could mean travel to another country and engaging in homestays where you live, eat, and spend time in dialogue with locals, or it could mean finding local cultural centers and events in which you can be immersed, giving up what you normally do and trying something new. School districts, nonprofits, and universities offer training programs with a focus on cultural difference and working with diverse groups, many of which have moved online so that the options are abundant. Stepping outside of your comfort zone and attending cross-cultural films, plays, and other artistic exhibits will help you to reflect on and negotiate cultural differences in both personal and professional ways.

Global Classrooms

Why should we create global classrooms, that is, learning spaces that adopt culturally relevant pedagogies in order to support student learning, develop intercultural competencies, and motivate teachers and students to produce critically conscious global citizens? We must do this to meet the needs of our students. "The responsibilities of the teacher have dramatically shifted over the past decade to include preparing students for a complex, interconnected world" (Tichnor-Wagner et al., 2019, p. 1). According to Shaklee and Baily (2012), at least 75 percent of teachers in the United States are White, Anglo-European females, and less than 10 percent of K–12 teachers in the United States speak a language other than English. Because boundaries are dissolving between the local and the global, schools in the US have an increasing number of international students and English learners (ELs), and the biggest challenges of our time (such as climate change and immigration) are interconnected. Therefore, classrooms should reflect and contribute to interconnection and interdependence.

During the last decade, we have worked with teachers as we explored and offered various ways to internationalize classrooms (Bender-Slack, 2019). Of course, the work in each classroom must begin with you, the teacher. How will you bring the world into your classroom so that students see a global relevance to the work they do, whether they are answering math problems or engaging in a science experiment?

What does it mean to integrate global awareness and knowledge into critical literacy practices? How does our curricula and instruction differ if we center global rather than local needs, events, and spaces? The world is in a constant state of flux, creating openings for disrupting the commonplace. The ever-shifting political, economic, and social landscape provides opportunities for seeing the world through multiple perspectives and examining the relationship between language and power—and how that impacts teaching and learning. As teachers, we must remain alert and dedicated to supporting the intercultural growth of our students so that educators at all grade levels are creating learning spaces "where all students feel welcome, all students can learn, and global differences are addressed and shared in order to capitalize on the richness of the classroom's various cultures and backgrounds" (Bender-Slack, 2019, p. 9).

What's Missing?

A concern that is/was on our minds is this: What would it take for students to feel more engaged, or to want to co-create curriculum and the related literacy events? Questions and conversations are a start. This can be based on the personal and cultural resources brought to the learning situation by teachers, students, and the wider learning community. But each community is different, and students are coming from a variety of them. For example, still present in Indigenous cultures in the Andean Mountain communities in Peru is the notion of *Ayni*. This Quechua word, *Ayni*, means reciprocity. It represents the idea that the individuals and their needs are embedded in a community so that if one person requires help constructing a house out of clay bricks, others in the community will collaborate in this endeavor, and so when the next person needs help with digging a well, the community will help, and so on. It quite literally translates as "today for you, tomorrow for me." This sense of mutualism recognizes the interdependency necessary in thriving communities. With the individualistic ideology present in the US, and indeed what the country was founded on, the sense of mutualism and interdependency is missing—and that is within the local community. It comes, then, as no surprise that identifying and acting on a feeling of responsibility for those across the globe is often lacking.

Another oft-missing component is humility. While the history classes, political parties, and news stations have taught patriotism and even nationalism through describing the US as "the best country on Earth" and "the most powerful country," and "the world leader," there hasn't been much room for cultural humility. One way to understand this is to be open to learning from other countries and cultures because they often do many things better than we do in the US. One example is literacy campaigns from across the globe. These literacy campaigns show global techniques and strategies, cultural humility, the importance of raising literacy rates, and how we take reading for granted; they complicate how we teach reading and show the importance of small group size, that power and education is not just about going to school, that everyone fails from time to time, and how political literacy is.

Lastly, due to a common disinterest and superiority with regard to learning other languages, we are missing an appreciation for linguistic diversity both in and outside of schools. Since so much of culture is embedded in language, this becomes a hindrance for truly understanding other cultures. Moreover, lack of linguistic diversity limits the learning that can occur in schools and what students from different and diverse backgrounds can learn from each other. For example, linguistic diversity can be an asset to reading and writing workshops in that it opens up the possibility of incorporating a larger number of texts and a greater variety of literacy events.

We embrace Muhammad's (2020) assertion that "we live in a period where there's no time for 'urgent-free pedagogy.' Our instructional pursuits must be honest, bold, raw, unapologetic, and responsive to the social times" (p. 54). Perhaps first identifying what is missing from our instruction, our perspectives, and our experiences will help us take that sense of urgency and channel our energies in the direction toward transformation. That is our hope.

SAMPLE CCCCS

Imagine it! Students and teachers weaving in various disciplines to their inquiry about global matters. Here are sample CCCCs that embrace moving students through Applebee's notion of an integrated curriculum toward a global perspective. The following CCCCs include the overarching and subquestions that lead to yearlong conversations, building to reflective and meaningful learning by engaging in relevant, globally focused literacy events.

Envisioned and designed by teacher candidate Morgan (Clinton) Schutte, this CCCC (table 5.1) asked the overarching question: *How can we make connections on a global scale?*

Designed by teacher candidate Erika Vickers, this CCCC (table 5.2) proposed the following overarching question: *What does it mean to be a global citizen and how does my life really effect those in other parts of the world?*

Table 5.1. Morgan (Clinton) Schutte's CCCC

Making Connections on a Global Scale	Books/Materials	Assignments
First Quarter **Connecting to Yourself** Students will be encouraged to reflect on their own lives and who they are as a person. **Genre Focus:** Poetry and Memoir	*The Honest Truth* by Dan Gemeinhart This is a story about a boy who has cancer and decides to run away to climb a mountain, but instead realizes the importance of his life. Collections of memoirs online	"I Am" poem using template from ReadWriteThink Unpacking your earliest memory—students will brainstorm ideas about their earliest memory and write a memoir (around two pages in length) about this memory.
Second Quarter **Connecting Locally** Students will begin to look beyond themselves and onto their surrounding community. **Genre Focus:** Persuasive, Informative, and Argumentative Writing	The *New York Times* article entitled "401 Prompts for Argumentative Writing" gives examples of topics students could write about. Local newspapers and news clips that show current issues occurring in their community. Commercials directed at different age/ gender groups.	Students will either brainstorm a topic that impacts their school/community, or research a topic, that will work as their argumentative focus for the quarter. Students will research a topic they are passionate about in their community (homelessness, school lunch programs, bullying, etc.) and create a multimedia project surrounding the topic. This project will need to include a piece of writing, as well as an artistic aspect such as a drawing, a video, or a short skit. The artistic aspect will be the student's choice.
Third Quarter **Connecting Societally** Students will start to look at society in general and how it impacts them personally, as well as those around them. **Genre Focus:** Fiction	*The Giver,* by Lois Lowry Looks at society and the repression of feelings/thoughts and how to counteract that society. Short stories such as *One Green Apple,* which depict American societal norms and social issues like racism.	Students will begin to examine societal norms and shifts that lead to social justice issues. They will focus on reading and analyzing works of fiction that show a negative impact on the world through societal changes.
Fourth Quarter **Connecting Globally** Students will expand their outlook even further by looking at issues on a global scale, opposed to personally or locally. **Genre Focus:** Nonfiction	"He Named Me Malala" film and/or *I Am Malala* Stories of young activists such as Payal Jangid, Malala, etc. Trip to the Freedom Center in downtown Cincinnati	Students will read stories about young activists who are using their struggles and situations for social change. Students will examine works of nonfiction to read about real-life social activists that deny social norms to help others.

Table 5.2. Erika Vicker's CCCC

Quarter One	Quarter Two	Quarter Three	Quarter Four
What role do I play in the world around me?	How do others live their lives in the world today?	How do rights of citizens compare in places across the world? How do governmental systems stifle or support individual rights of citizens?	What will I do to help further the rights of citizens across the world and to stay informed about issues in the world around me? What does it mean to be a global citizen?
Assignment: Students will construct family trees, which demonstrate their nationality. Students will give oral presentations on how culture has impacted their family traditions, beliefs, and values. *Text:* Students will look through magazines to find images of things that dominate American culture.	*Text:* Students will read *Esperanza Rising*, which will expose them to Mexican American culture. *Assignment:* Students will write a short informational speech in which they compare some cultural traditions from the text with those that they practice with their own families. *Text:* Students will view pictures of people from third-world countries.	*Text:* Students will review the amendments to the Constitution to familiarize themselves with the rights they have as citizens in America's democracy. *Assignment:* Students will create a constitution of their own in small groups, which requires them to take away liberties given by the amendments to the Constitution and add rights to a leader that would not be allowed under a democracy.	*Text:* Black Eyed Peas and Justin Timberlake's song "Where Is the Love?" *Assignment:* Students will write in their journals about how this song is related to the themes they discussed in this unit, and what they believe it means to be a global citizen. *Text:* Students will read the workers' rights section of a job application.

Assignment: Students will make collages with these images and write a poem about how they feel the media makes one feel about himself or herself, and whether media encourages them to think about others or just themselves.

Text: Clothing. Students will bring in an article of clothing that was made in a different country.

Assignment: Students will be expected to do research, referencing their social studies textbook and other resources, on the process clothing goes through from nature, to manufacturer, to marketer, to store, to one's own home. They will create a flow chart to depict how their article of clothing probably reached their own hands. The teacher will lead a discussion on the social injustices that go along with sweatshops and other such institutions that play a part in this system.

Assignment: Students will write personal narratives from the perspective of one of the people in the pictures, to process through what type of life a person with less economic resources experiences every day.

Text: Students will read firsthand accounts of immigration stories. One will be a current story from Latin America, another will be a current story from Africa, and another will be from the colonization period in America with the first settlers.

Assignment: Students will focus on one of the current articles and explain in an essay why that person immigrated, including the social and economic situations involved. The student will also include the personal emotions the individual experienced, and discuss whether they desired to immigrate or not. This will help students realize that immigration does not always follow the public's stereotypes of job-stealing illegals.

Text: Students will read current news articles about religious intolerance and the lack of voting rights of others around the world.

Assignment: Students will videotape themselves as newscasters, giving reports on the news articles they found. This will demonstrate how the world's inequalities in democratic rights all coexist today.

Text: Students will listen to Bob Marley's song "Get Up, Stand Up."

Assignment: Students will write editorial articles for a newspaper, which encourage people to stand up for their rights. They will identify and explain the type of government they feel best promotes people's rights.

Assignment: Students will write letters to their senators about what they feel the state should do to support immigrant workers' rights, so that they may be treated as fairly as US citizens.

Assignment: Students will each research a nonprofit agency in the United States that works with workers in other countries. They will write a short paper on how this agency works to tackle an issue that puts people at a disadvantage in the area where they come from, either economically or socially.

Activity: The class will brainstorm together what type of agency they would like to donate to. There will be a walkathon to raise money for this group.

Assignment: Each week, students will have to bring in current event articles about social justice issues from other areas of the world. These will be presented in class to keep students up-to-date on global issues.

Teacher Summary

Students will begin the year by exploring their place in the world, considering how they participate in media, what their specific cultural identity is, and the level in which they interact with the world around them. Then, students will be exposed to a few different cultures and economic situations through readings and pictures. They will see how others live and how different their point of reference is, given where they come from. Students will compare these thought processes and lifestyles to their own. Third quarter, students will go a step deeper and learn about the rights of citizens in different places around the world and will compare them to the rights they have themselves in the United States. In the last quarter of the year, students will define for themselves what they believe it means to be a global citizen. Students will be encouraged to come up with ways to stay knowledgeable about the world around them and to involve themselves in groups that help create a society that considers the needs of all people.

Designed by teacher candidate Katherine Kinney, this CCCC (table 5.3) proposes the following overarching question: *What is your place in the wider world?*

HELPFUL SUGGESTIONS

Upon our writing of this chapter, we offer the following suggestions:

Think in Daily Acts

There is a lot that you can do daily to raise your global awareness and increase your global knowledge. Consider your current routine, like the coffee you drink and the food chain of which you are a part, and learn about the farms that provide that to you. Download geography apps that help you identify countries and capital cities across the continents. Change the sources of your daily news. We switched from a national morning news program to BBC and within six months could easily and naturally discuss topics from around the globe. It is amazing how your perspective changes when you choose to de-center the US and local news!

Engage in Personal Interactions

Work on projects and socialize with people from different cultures. One way to do this yourself is to engage in language learning. Since so few teachers (less than 10 percent) in the US have learned another language, understanding

Table 5.3. Katherine Kinney's CCCC: From a Part to the Whole

Quarter	Topics	Assignments and Resources
First	*You* • Who are you? • What shaped your worldview? • What are the most important things in your life?	*You* About students, their values, and what makes them unique, including their own histories and challenges. Book: Mafi, T. (2017). *Furthermore*. Penguin Group USA. Other: poems by various authors, Townshend, P. (1978). "Who Are You." On *Who Are You*. MCA Records. (1977, October 4). Assignments: A collections of poems about you, your family, and your thoughts and a short story about an event that changed your life or how you view yourself
Second	*Us* • Who are we? • What events define our community? • How do we decide who is part of "us"?	*Us* About families, communities, nations, and what makes them work or not work together. Book: Anderson, J. D. (2017). *Posted*. S. L: Walden Pond Press. Other: historic information about the community, Kennedy, E. (1996). "Say You'll Be There." On *Spice* [CD]. Absolute. Assignments: A photo essay about important people or places in the community being studied including commentary about why they are important and a brochure or poster to inform others.
Third	*Them* • Who do we label as "them"? • How do we treat others unlike us? • Why has this been the case?	*Them* About who we "other," how we treat them, and why. Book: Stockett, K. (2011). *The Help*. Berkley Books. Other: Lewis, J., & Aydin, A. (2013, 2015, 2016). *March* (Vols. 1–3, March) (N. Powell, IL). Marietta, G. A.: Top Shelf Productions., Meeropol, A. (1939). "Strange Fruit" [Recorded by B. Holiday]. On *Strange Fruit* [Vinyl recording]. Commodore. (1939, April 20). Assignments: Research and a long-form essay paper about a minority group including the history of their struggle for acceptance and the current equality of rights (or not) [Crit. Lit.]
Fourth	*World* • How can we move from "us" and "them" to a more collective worldview? • What is your place in the wider world? • What can we do to help others?	*World* About how to embrace diversity, stop the cycle of violence, and become better individuals in the process. Book: Diaz, A. (2018). *Only Road*. Simon & Schuster. Other: Garraud, J., Guetta, D., & Carré, J. C. (2002). "Just a Little More Love" [Recorded by C. Willis]. On *Just a Little More Love* [CD]. David Guetta, Joachim Garraud. (2001–2002) Assignments: Advocacy campaign to raise awareness about a social justice issue based on student choice. Students will be taking this opportunity to organize, write, or design pieces to advocate for change, both on their own and with a small group.

English learners in their classrooms may be a challenge, if not impossible. Another suggestion for teachers and students is to engage in specific cultural site visits where you can interact with others and learn about diverse cultural experiences. Teachers can also plan virtual exchanges with schools from a different country where students can speak virtually, but synchronously, with others from around the globe.

Locate New Texts

One text that you can use to engage in transdisciplinary teaching is the *United Nations Sustainability Goals*. This allows for the teacher to organize planning, teaching, and student learning around the construction of meaning in the context of real-world problems or themes such as climate change, war, and poverty. For example, in a recent of virtual exchange experience, teacher candidates from disciplines as diverse as journalism, law, and education discussed issues and created projects around themes such as water crisis, systemic inequalities, global citizenship, and healthcare.

DECONSTRUCTING THE CURRENT SYSTEM OF INSTITUTIONALIZED POWER AND EXISTING IDEOLOGIES OF CURRICULA

The potential to change the world lies in education, but more often than not, schooling perpetuates the status quo and the inherent unjust and oppressive structures. Kress and Lake (2013) define radical hope as "a refusal to accept the world, with all its pain and ugliness, as it is. Yet, at the same time, it carries with it a responsibility to act upon our desire for a different future" (p. xiv). Accepting the responsibility to confront injustices is a task teachers cannot take lightly. It is part of the democratic project, and it is clear our democracy is faltering. When teaching for social justice, the role of the teacher changes. Instead, teachers are activists and students are change makers. Both are working toward very real transformation to make the world more equitable and just. There is a concurrent, dual commitment to academic success and critical consciousness, which is made all the more difficult because "the field of education is anchored in White rage, especially public education" (Love, 2020, p. 21). Curricular tools of Whiteness "use a variety of strategies to socialize students to internalize existing racist ideologies, ensuring that racial hierarchies are maintained through the education system" (Picower, 2021, p. 26). These tools include exclusively White curricula, blame dodging, minimization of injustices, conflation of equal with equitable, dependence on viewing the world through the White gaze, embedded stereotypes of racial differences and deficiencies, and racist policies and procedures.

We can disrupt schooling as business-as-usual by interrogating the fiction of Whiteness as a way to help readers of all races "think critically about how race functions systemically and often subconsciously to privilege people with certain perceived skin traits" (Beech, 2020, p. 3).

In this way, all teachers can confront their own complicity in White supremacy, which is the "racist ideology that is based upon the belief that white people are superior . . . and that therefore . . . should be dominant . . . which extend to how systems and institutions are structured to uphold this white dominance" (Saad, 2020, p. 12). Due to the history of colonialization, this White dominance is global in nature. The flip side of White dominance in schooling is the violence it perpetuates on students of color. For example, we need to confront those who profit from dark suffering (injuring students of color) such as the testing, prison, and textbook industries as well as charter schools and the super-predator corporate school reformers (Love, 2020).

Another way to disrupt the commonplace is to focus on language and/in community rather than privileging individuals over the whole. When traveling with students during study abroad programs, we emphasize making all decisions for the good of the group. So if a student is thinking, I want to risk drinking the tap water, they pause and think, if I do that and get sick, that could impact our group plans to hike Machu Picchu tomorrow, so is this decision for the good of the group? "If learning does not strengthen our bonds, does not move us in the direction of equity, does not improve our chances of living healthy, fulfilled lives, then why do it" (Bender-Slack, 2020, p. 1)? We advocate for using a critical, antiracist lens that focuses on equity in radical and authentic ways through a global perspective/lens.

While literacy involves cognitive processes, it is also embedded in social practices, which means justice and equity issues are sure to arise. Literacy events, including reading and writing, do not occur in isolation or outside of larger contexts. In schools, for example, literacies are linked to inequities, such as those involving race, gender, immigration, varied abilities, and economic equality. We resist the popular notion that a standardized curriculum evens the playing field for students because it negates the fact that students come to every learning task with a variety of background knowledge, skills, experiences, and interests. Standardization, by its very essence, is "antithetical to diversity" chiefly because it suggests that students live, learn, and operate in homogeneous environments, with equal opportunities provided to them, and resources evenly distributed across the board (Milner, 2010). Antiracist and abolitionist approaches may provide a solution. For example, "abolitionist teaching stands in solidarity with parents and fellow teachers opposing standardized testing, English-only education, racist teachers, arming teachers with guns, and turning schools into prisons. Abolitionist teaching supports and teaches from the space that Black Lives Matter, all Black Lives Matter, and affirms Black folx' humanity" (Love, 2020, p. 12). This type of teaching is founded in our shared humanity, because when one suffers and struggles, the community suffers and struggles.

We believe that taking a global approach is about interconnectedness and interdependence. We advocate that teachers model being global citizens by building a global network and leading with hope. This cannot be done in isolation. We strive toward creating antiracist schools based in intersectional justice that immerse students in places where love, healing, and joy are possible.

Parting Thought

If, as Love says, freedom is a practice rather than a possession or a state of being, in what ways do we engage in that practice for and with students?

Chapter 6

Obstacles to Critical Literacy Planning

Shifting from Unit to Lesson Planning

Overarching question: How might educators maintain a "big picture" perspective while concurrently managing the multiple ongoing classroom conversations and individual lesson plans?

Big Ideas:

- Fully embracing *knowledge-in-action* allows and encourages both teacher and students to enter into relevant, dynamic, and critical conversations within the vibrant and living traditions of disciplinary discourse.
- Teacher candidates and in-service educators can learn to see past individual lessons and focus on the power and potential of a "big picture" perspective of their instructional units.
- Moving from "big picture" instructional planning to organization of individual lesson plans can be challenging.

KNOWLEDGE-IN-ACTION AS A FOUNDATION FOR THE "BIG PICTURE"

Applebee (1996) indicates that traditions are the "knowledge-in-action" out of which we construct our realities as we know and perceive them, and that to honor such traditions we must reconstrue our curriculum to focus on knowledge-in-action rather than knowledge-out-of-context. We have discussed knowledge-in-action at great length in this book and have embraced it as a way to support "classroom talk" and contextualize what we choose to read, write, view, visually represent, and do in a classroom as part of a larger disciplinary context.

For Applebee, traditions are the "tools" we use for understanding, making sense of, and changing our world. As literacy educators, these tools include—but are not limited to—the consumption of texts (reading and viewing), the production of texts (writing and graphically representing), and the linguistic expressions (listening and speaking) of our understanding of texts. Active and engaged participation in these traditions are required for individuals to create meaning for themselves and to fully participate in collective meaning making. That is to say that the many genres of language we use on a daily basis are embedded in the traditions of our everyday life and in concert with other members of those discourse communities. We learn and utilize semantics (content), syntax (structure), and pragmatics (purpose) in order to understand and be understood in a host of different social situations: on the bus, at our job, within our family, at our religious/spiritual gatherings, in a restaurant, on a sports field, and with our friends. In these cases, we learn *by doing*, by active engagement, and through repeated opportunities for exposure and practice.

Likewise, when we consider schools, it's important to remember that what we are really requiring students to do is master new traditions of discourse. Our goal is not for them to learn about those discourses but rather to engage in them *by doing*. This *doing* looks different in each of the disciplines, doing history versus doing math, and even within the disciplines themselves. For example, *doing biology* differs from *doing chemistry* or *doing physics*. In order to plan for a curriculum that embraces knowledge-in-action, we must consider the traditions that support the literate behavior we wish to see in each disciplinary conversation that our students are expected to engage.

WHAT'S MISSING?

Our focus on the "big picture" has been intentional. When we lose the "big picture," we lose the overarching sense of direction and purpose that guides our planning and helps us to remember that the lessons we plan are meant to be transaction oriented, not transmission focused. That is to say that we are not teaching *at* students, we are facilitating learning *with* students. Some have used the phrase "guide on the side," rather than the "sage on the stage," to remind us that how we position ourselves matters when planning for critical literacy classroom conversations. A "sage on stage" is an instructor who lectures almost exclusively, who has the philosophy that she has knowledge to give learners who would benefit from this. A "guide on the side" is a facilitator who assists learners in discovering knowledge and acquiring skills, steering them in ways that would help them help themselves (Morrison, 2014). This, in turn, requires students to become active, not passive, learners, who are expected to take responsibility for their own learning through full engagement and the use of literate practices.

Avoiding the "sage on the stage" stance is difficult. Although we are now teachers, our experiences as students shape our understanding of what it means to teach and what it means to learn, and the pull toward the traditional power structure is strong and enticing. However, the traditions that surround transmission-focused teaching and learning do not support the idea that students can share the power of curriculum development in important and meaningful ways. A standards-based mentality, coupled with demands of various stakeholders (districts, parents, community leaders, politicians), can also drive teachers to adopt pedagogical strategies that appear, on the surface, to produce quick results and "success" based on quantitative measures such as test scores.

In our own work with teacher candidates, we have found that, while many candidates understand and welcome the idea of creating a transformative space in the classroom using critical literacy and curricular conversations, putting these ideas into practice can create quite a challenge. Even those able to conceptualize and plan a well-designed unit for that purpose can struggle when shifting to an individual lesson plan that is supposed to be nested in a larger conversation that is student driven.

SAMPLE UNIT/LESSON PLAN #1

We are going to return to Isabel whose unit plan, "What makes a great society?" was featured in chapter 3. We want to look at the ways in which the "big picture" perspective she adopted so well in her unit plan plays out when she begins to design an individual lesson. In order to ensure that teacher candidates understood previous discussions regarding curricular conversations and critical literacy, we asked students to respond to two questions: (1) What is curriculum? And (2) what is critical literacy?

In response to the question, "What is curriculum?" Isabel wrote:

Curriculum originates from our traditions of scholarship in the different disciplines (mathematics, science, literature, etc.). Its goal is to provide a framework for the body of knowledge and skills that students should acquire. . . . Ideally the curriculum for our classrooms can be set up through a series of questions that help students engage in the current discussions within respective disciplines.

In this response, it is clear that Isabel understands the significance of the overarching question, the individual questions that feed back into the overarching question, and the significance of supporting students in ongoing and contemporary conversations of disciplinary traditions. Likewise, when asked the question, "What is critical literacy?" Isabel indicated:

> Critical literacy involves valuing students' prior knowledge (their personal and cultural backgrounds) and using it to help them make connections to social issues. They should be able to, with some scaffolding and practice, use their knowledge to analyze and synthesize data and come up with justice oriented solutions to problems. Critical literacy cuts across the personal and the social and sets students up with a focus and bias toward action for social justice. It requires using different analytical skills to interpret and analyze literature to inform this bias toward action.

Again, it appears that Isabel appreciates the basic tenets of critical literacy based not only on this response, but her comprehension of these ideas is also evident in her unit plan, which shows clear indication of being integrated, recursive, and rooted in action toward equity and justice. Indeed, her unit plan was exemplary in that almost every aspect of it led to action meant to prioritize social justice.

In addition to studying critical literacy and curricular conversation theory and developing a CCCC, teacher candidates in this methods course were also asked to submit a "critical literacy" lesson that they developed in their practicum courses. As a methods course connected to a practicum experience, we wanted to ensure that students were transferring the ideas from the course to their praxis in the field. Isabel submitted a lesson plan on connotation and denotation. This lesson plan can be seen below (table 6.1).

There is a great deal of positive feedback that we can offer this teacher candidate about this lesson plan. The lesson affords both small group collaboration and whole group discussion opportunities, providing opportunities for the meaningful discourse that is central to transaction-oriented teaching and learning. It uses real-world examples to highlight the lesson's potential relevance to students' everyday lives. It is active, providing students with engaging and meaningful practice that helps them make connections and evaluate their own work as it relates to the skill currently being taught. The students use five of the six language arts—reading, writing, viewing, speaking, and listening. It implements a lesson cycle (Hunter, 1982) that includes an introduction (setting the focus, objective, and purpose), direct instruction (explanation, modeling, and monitoring), guided practice, a formative assessment of mastery, some independent practice, another formative assessment,

Table 6.1. Isabel's Lesson Plan

Subject	Language Arts (English)
Grade level	7
Context of the Lesson	Prior to this lesson, students will have learned the meanings of denotation and connotation. During this lesson, students will review the meaning of denotation and connotation and practice analyzing the impact of a word's connotation on a text's meaning and tone. They will also have the opportunity to practice using words with different connotations to convey a particular meaning or tone in their own writing. Following this lesson, students will continue to apply their skills in analyzing the connotation of words and their impact on text. They will carefully choose words with particular connotations to construct specific meaning in the text that they write.
Standard	Explain the concept of connotation and analyze the impact of connotation on a text's meaning and tone. Strand: Reading Standards for informational text Domain: Craft and Structure Determine the meaning of words and phrases as they are used in a text, including figurative, connotative, and technical meanings; analyze the impact of a specific word choice on meaning and tone
Objective	Practice analyzing the connotation of words and their impact on text; practice selecting word with specific connotations to use in their own texts to evoke a certain feeling from their reader.

Procedure/ Sequence of Activities	Introduction (5 mins.):
	 • Discuss the meaning of the famous quote: "That which we call a rose by any other name would smell as sweet."
	  • Discuss what students think Shakespeare meant.
	  • Tell the class they will decide if the quote is true or not by reviewing connotation and denotation.
	 • Ask the class if they remember and can explain the difference between connotation and denotation.
	  • Clarify responses by explaining that denotation is the explicit or direct meaning of a word or expression and connotation is the associated or secondary meaning of a word or expression in addition to its explicit meaning; it is the emotions or human reactions that come from a word.
	 • Review examples on the board including:
	  • *Modern* (denotation is belonging to recent times; connotation is new, up-to-date, and experimental)
	  • *Home* (denotation is place where one lives; connotation is security, family, love, comfort)
	 Activity #1 Connotations in Literature (5 mins.)
	 • Hand out worksheets with book titles and graphic organizers and have children (with a partner) analyze the connotation of the word *chicken* in book titles; allow students to report out why they think the authors chose to use *chicken* in the title in the particular way they did.

Activity #2 Connotations in Everyday Life (5 mins.)
- Provide students with list of team names. Students will be asked to give a definition (denotation) of each word, as well as their reaction (connotation) to the word and consider why these names were chosen (e.g., team pride, sounds athletic, great for marketing, etc.). List includes Dallas Cowboys, New York Giants, Detroit Lions, Chicago Bears.
- Project Igor's home page (branding agency) and discuss how team names might attract and inspire fans.

Activity #3 Connotation in Everyday Life (5 mins.)
- Tell students that they will not have a chance to create their own product names. Working in groups for three to four minutes, they will create a name for the product they are assigned and explain why they chose the name that they did by explaining the name's denotation, connotation, and what they meant to accomplish/how they will influence people
- Pull the whole class together and have the students report out.

Closing (1–2 mins.)
- Go back to Shakespeare's quote: "That which we call a rose by any other name would smell as sweet."
- Have students consider their original answer. Would, for example, a rose still smell as sweet f we called it a "stinkweed"? Would it be as popular if it had a different name?

Assessment   Formative assessments (these will not be graded) include:
- Analyzing the connotative meaning of words in book titles and team names
- Explaining what emotions these connotations evoke in the reader and the author's purpose
- Select a name for a product (a new smart phone) and explain why they chose the name, what its connotation is, and what emotion they intend to evoke in the reader/buyer and why

Materials/   Mac Book, projector, white board and markers, *Chicken* handout, activity handouts
Resources

Technology   Mac Book, projector, Ignore text on advertisements: http://www.igorinternational.com/process.html
Integration   Ideas for this lesson were taken from:
                    http://www.readwritethink.org/classroom-resources/lesson-plans/avalanche-aztek-bravada-connotation-75.html?tab=1#tabs
                    http://www.cholastic.com/teachers/lesson-plan/whats-name-0

Critical   This lesson involves critical literacy because it gets students to consciously engage by paying attention to the language we
Literacy in   use. It also encourages them to understand and think how knowledge is constructed.
This Lesson

and a closing that reflects back to the introduction, allowing students to see connections within the individual features of the lesson itself.

That said, most of what is covered in the class is teacher designed and standard driven, usurping much of the students' power in co-creating curriculum in an organic way. The teacher spends a great deal of time creating a "sage on the stage" stance: the teacher has come up with the examples to explore in each activity, the products to be named, and the considerations to contemplate, which is typical of teacher candidates who are highly concerned with classroom management and control. There are few obvious connections to previous learning in the unit or future learning in or outside of the classroom. This limits both the recursive nature of the lesson and the connection to a broader purpose or overarching question, as well as limiting the ways in which students can enter in the traditions of literary analysis. (This may be due to only being in the field twice a week, thus being unaware of how her topic connects with pervious learning, but the relevancy should have been addressed.) While the teacher does take the time to contextualize what has occurred prior to this lesson and how she envisions future lessons, there is nothing in the procedure that indicates that it is made explicit to the students. The lesson is self-contained without comprehension regarding how this lesson, for example, connects to the overarching purpose of the unit save for a casual nod to the students' previous reading and future writing.

Perhaps more interesting is that it is submitted as representative of a critical literacy lesson for older readers. We recognize that it contains some elements of critical literacy such as consciously engaging and taking responsibility to question or inquire, yet the heart of critical literacy, including focusing on sociopolitical issues and taking action to promote social justice, is not raised or even suggested. Understanding, for example, how the process of product branding and marketing based on connotation (as represented by the candidate's quick dip into the Igor website) is an issue of equity and justice would be a better representation of critically literate teaching. The candidate might have also considered issues of equity and justice by requiring students to inquire into the differences in connotations derived by individual students based on their background, culture, and experience. For example, why might Student A have a different reaction to teams such as the Cleveland Indians, Kansas City Chiefs, Atlanta Braves, Golden State Warriors, and the Chicago Blackhawks than Student B? The lesson plan itself, while quite insightful on so many levels, misses several opportunities to push the boundaries and open more fully the spaces offered at the intersection of critical literacy and classroom conversations.

We must recognize and note that this teacher candidate, along with many practicing teachers, may feel constrained by time limits (as indicated by the amount of time for each activity within the lesson plan). Likewise, this teacher candidate, as previously mentioned, was in a practicum setting, teaching the content assigned to them by the mentor teacher and perhaps even using materials suggested or required by the teacher, the school, or the district. Teacher candidates often have limited, if any, flexibility in designing lessons that fit into a broader scope of learning, yet it provides issues of power, control, equity, and justice that we encourage all teachers, especially those with their own classrooms, to consider.

SAMPLE UNIT/LESSON PLAN #2

Let's now take a look at Emma Bruggeman's content area lesson plan (table 6.2). On the surface, this lesson plan, like Isabel's, appears very teacher centered, especially in the procedure. The teacher directs the lesson. She requires them to write the "I Can" statement, she explicitly teaches the new math vocabulary, and she guides the students through the mathematical processes of converting percentages to decimals, multiplying decimals and whole numbers, and determining markup, markdown, and retail process.

Like Isabel, Emma also encourages small-group and partner collaboration to practice the skill, as well as to utilize peer teaching to move toward mastery, which allows them a chance to engage in disciplinary and academic discourse within the context of the lesson. It has a "sage on the stage" position for at least part of the lesson, switching to a "guide on the side" stance when they begin working in small groups, allowing the peers to instruct one another to encourage a deeper understanding, especially given the large number of students who are learning English as a second language. She also uses observational checklists as a formative assessment, providing opportunities for students to demonstrate what they know through performance rather than through regurgitation or formal test taking. She focuses on the real-world aspect of the skill by providing examples of how the students will apply this skill in meaningful and relevant ways, including the use of word problems that are not only focused on the math skill but also inclusive of a social justice idea.

One example she provides that should spark an interesting classroom discussion is the following: A local nonprofit organization is selling popcorn to raise money for hurricane relief. The organization paid $4 per bag for the popcorn and sold it for $5 a bag. What was the percent markup on each bag of popcorn?

This teacher candidate also wrote an interesting reflection that helps us to better understand the critical literacy and curricular conversation implications. The addendum to her lesson plan shows that Emma has a deep understanding of the sociopolitical implications of her mathematics lessons

Table 6.2. Emma's Lesson Plan

Subject	Math
Grade level	7
Student background and demographics	A private, Catholic school located in an urban center of a mid-sized Midwestern city. Enrollment, which includes all students from preschool through eighth grade, is 219 students. They also accept the State's Educational Choice Voucher for grades K–8. Over 80 percent of the students are Latino and come from Spanish-speaking houses. In these households, students are the primary English speakers of the family, and English is spoken at the school.
Standard	Analyze proportional relationships and use them to solve real-world and mathematical problems.
	7.RP.3 Use proportional relationships to solve multistep ratio and percent problems.
	DI.6–8.6 I interact with people who are similar to and different from me, and I show respect to all people.
	SJ Standard J.12. Students will recognize unfairness on the individual level (e.g., biased speech) and injustice at the institutional or systemic level (e.g., discrimination).
Objective	Calculate markups, markdowns, retail prices, and discount prices, and represent them using equations of the form $y = kx$
Procedure/sequence of activities	I Can statement: I Can calculate markups and markdowns
	• Students take out math notebook and start writing "I Can" statement—students finish writing the I Can statement, teacher reads the I Can statement aloud, students join the teacher in reading the I Can statement aloud.
	• Teacher highlights vocabulary (markup, markdown).
	• Work through problems together—converting percentages to decimals, multiplying decimals and whole numbers to determine markup, markdown, or retail price.
	• Students work with table groups to figure out problems independently and teach each other or discuss where they are confused.
Assessment	Formative assessments (these will not be graded) include:
	• Observational checklist
	• Circulating around the room to assist students
Materials/resources	HMHCO seventh-grade math textbook and teacher's edition
	Pencil, math notebooks (which include the "I Can" statements as well as definitions with examples), and CleverTouch board
Critical literacy in math	Mathematics is a language itself. In order to understand the problem, one must understand the symbols, variables, numbers, and vocabulary. To grow this knowledge, students involve themselves in discourse about the subject and learn from their peers as well as ask questions to better understand the content.

Chapter 6

and the ways in which it can be embedded into a larger CCCC unit that has a guiding purpose. The "I Can" statement, at first glance, appears to have little to no connection to what we were requiring, but, in fact, it is central to her understanding of her ESL students' need for the building of background knowledge, the vocabulary required to enter into the disciplinary discourse, and her desire to connect the lesson to real-world inequities and injustices. In Emma's reflection, she states:

> Math is a language in and of itself. Students have to understand the language and vocabulary in math in order to fully comprehend and engage in discourse on the topic . . . I consciously engage students in the content by deconstructing the vocabulary terms for the lesson we are learning . . . [because] . . . some students may have little to no schema on these words so I first asked students to briefly talk to each other and tell me where they have heard these words and in what context. Students noted that they had heard these terms related to clothes, food, and items such as books. Since this module is filled with real-world scenarios that include tips, taxes, percent increase, and percent decrease, it was important to first engage students in how the content relates to them and the real world. This . . . help[s] them realize the content is not a math lesson that does not build upon itself. Instead, this math is used every day in stores that sell things like clothes, food, and books like the students stated. . . . Overall, the students in my class are actively learning content by breaking down what each term means in order to properly solve an equation and for us as a class to communicate using math "language." . . . The SJ standard that stands out to me and seems to fit for this lesson is DI.6–8.6 "I interact with people who are similar to and different from me, and I show respect to all people." With this lesson, a real-world scenario can be incorporated that some people can only buy things that are marked down because of their budget. Whereas some people do not hesitate when they notice an item has been marked up and can afford it. Being able to appreciate differences between people show others respect and interact with diverse individuals at the grocery, clothing store, mall, restaurant, etc. Recognizing perspectives and SES can also be incorporated for this lesson. I could incorporate a budget for students and create a "shop" for them and they can only spend a certain amount based on marked up and marked down items.

HELPFUL SUGGESTIONS

Upon our writing of this chapter, we offer the following suggestions:

Create Lesson Plans Rooted in Your CCCC

Once you have envisioned and designed your CCCC, continue to use that—and the curriculum as conversation intersection with critical literacy—as your inspiration when designing lessons. The CCCC is only the first step; it's the big picture. The actual lesson planning is how we implement that vision, when as they say, "the rubber meets the road." If you feel like you are doing what you've always done when engaging in instructional planning, then the CCCC work has been for naught. There should be a veritable shift in your instructional planning with a focus on critical literacy practices with regard to teacher planning and student learning. You can use the following Self-Check Planning Organizer (table 6.3) as your critical literacy checklist.

Go Beyond the Classroom

All of this planning is very important because what we do in classrooms matters, but what we do in the larger school structure, the institutional policies and practices, matters too. We must also go beyond pedagogy for this to be radical and transformative. Embracing the big picture vision that we have advocated for throughout this book, Love (2020) also reminds us that the work is bigger:

> No type of pedagogy, however effective, can single-handedly remove the barriers of racism, discrimination, homophobia, segregation, Islamophobia, homelessness, access to college, and concentrated poverty, but antiracist pedagogy combined with grassroots organizing can prepare students and their families to demand the impossible in the fight for eradicating these persistent and structural barriers. (p. 19)

As teachers, push your work to be antiracist and transformative. Engage in difficult discussions. Be uncomfortable. Advocate for students of color, English learners, students experiencing poverty, and others who experience

Table 6.3. Self-Check Planning Organizer

Critical Literacy Practice	Evident (yes or no)	How/Where?
Being reflexive		
Entertaining alternate ways of being		
Taking responsibility		
Consciously engaging		
Disrupting the commonplace		
Interrogating multiple viewpoints		
Focusing on sociopolitical issues		
Taking action		
Moving between the personal and the social		

the violence of traditional US schools so that they can thrive instead. Get involved in grassroots organizations as members of your school communities who work in hope to meaningfully change the status quo while lifting each other up. Demand the impossible. Schooling has not changed because we have not transformed it.

DECONSTRUCTING THE CURRENT SYSTEM OF INSTITUTIONALIZED POWER AND EXISTING IDEOLOGIES OF CURRICULA

Oppression consolidates power to benefit people in the privileged group, and it operates on multiple levels. Oppression can be internal, interpersonal, cultural, and structural. What we are proposing is that planning and implementing transformative instruction may address internalized oppressions through reflections and engagement with texts and the interpersonal as students engage in conversations. The ultimate objective, however, is that we confront and dismantle the structural aspects of oppression—that is, how schools create and enact oppressive policies and processes.

Can you use the master's tools to dismantle the master's house? We believe we have to work both inside and outside the structural. In her seminal essay about transforming silence to action, Audre Lorde explains that "primarily for us all, it is necessary to teach by living and speaking those truths which we believe and know beyond understanding. Because in this way alone we can survive, by taking part in a process of life that is creative and continuing, that is growth" (Lorde, 2007, p. 43). Teachers can live and speak truths so that schools are more humane and just and equitable.

What suffering has schooling caused in the US? In what ways does it continue to oppress students of color? Love (2020) claims that if education is one of the principal tools used to maintain White supremacy and anti-immigrant hate, then teachers are an integral part in dismantling that.

Parting Thought

In your everyday lives, how are you either maintaining the current structure of White supremacy or dismantling it?

Chapter 7

Equity-Based Educational Planning

Moving toward Justice and Shared Power

Overarching question: How might teachers create hopeful, transformative classrooms that prioritize shared power?

Big Ideas:

- Progressive social change, both in and out of schools, must begin "in the trenches" where practitioners hone their craft and real curricula emerge.
- Policies implemented at the school, district, state, and federal level can affect curriculum development.
- Teachers have power within the classroom context to initiate transformative classroom discourse and pedagogy.

FINDING YOUR POWER IN CLASSROOM TEACHING

Education is not politically neutral. Schools have both hidden curricula and null curricula that represent subtle, but deeply influential, forces in the shaping of attitudes and beliefs. The hidden curriculum refers to the implicit academic, social, and cultural messages that students learn as a result of both the unwritten rules and unspoken expectations of teachers and schools, as well as the unofficial norms, behaviors, and values that are considered acceptable. While the visible curriculum includes those things that might show up in a course syllabus or lesson plans (e.g., the methods and materials of teaching

87

math, science, or languages), the hidden curriculum would not show up in course documents, yet it is what educators use to teach students how to behave, walk, talk, interact, and even what to wear. Teaching, for example, that students should raise their hand and wait to speak as part of an academic exchange isn't part of an official curriculum, yet it *is* part of what is taught in schools. These morals, norms, and power hierarchies are always part of the dominant culture in which all teaching and learning are situated. Students learn this information implicitly, even if explicit instruction is not directed to this end.

Likewise, the null curriculum represents that information that schools and teachers *don't* teach. According to Eisner, these can best be described as "the options students are not afforded, the perspectives they may never know about, much less be able to use, the concepts and skills that are not part of their intellectual repertoire" (Eisner, 1985, p. 107). A history teacher, for example, who covers the westward expansion but fails to discuss its impact on Indigenous tribes and the culture of Native Americans operates a null curriculum, denying students an opportunity to have certain experiences or to engage in specific interactions or discourses. What is omitted from the curriculum is, in a very real way, showing students what matters and what doesn't, regardless of whether or not it is intentional.

Literacy instruction, therefore, is also not politically neutral, but enmeshed in a network of social, political, cultural, and historical contexts. Literacy involves cognitive processes, but it is also embedded in social practices, meaning that justice and equity issues will emerge, and must be negotiated and confronted. Incorporating relevant social issues and reflecting their students' concerns are one way for teachers to plan for and embrace a *knowledge-in-action* that encourages students to enter into robust and relevant conversations that highlight the many ways individuals interact to create meaning and resolve conflict. Anything less than this leads to inevitable issues of inequity that arise when we fail to consider the socially mediated aspects of language processes.

Educators who recognize how and where both null and hidden curricula exist can find power for both themselves and their students in those empty and open spaces. Let's take the history teacher mentioned above who is expected to cover the westward expansion, perhaps using a district-provided textbook. If that teacher, for example, when recognizing the null curricula in failing to give voice to the Indigenous tribes' experience of the historical event, provides supplemental texts and materials, and allows his students to engage in critical conversations that embrace multiple perspectives, the students will be afforded opportunities and will hone skills that might have otherwise been overlooked or disregarded. The teacher makes spaces in the #curriculumsowhite. While the teacher will still have met the original learning outcome or addressed the required core standard, she will also have provided far more—the chance for students to explore, investigate, and consider all manner of interpretive possibility in the consumption and production of texts and in the critical "classroom talk" in which these activities are embedded.

Classroom work such as this has the potential, not only for transformative creation and implementation of curricula, but for life. Even simple decisions that occur "in the trenches of teaching" that start with a critical lens and ask whose interests are being served in the classroom and for what purpose can lead to major changes in both the experience of education and in the future life decisions made by those who engage in it. By taking a deep dive into the ways in which traditional curricular decisions prioritize the voices of the dominant culture, students and teachers begin to share the power needed to critically analyze and change them. Building curricula from the bottom up can inform future pedagogical practices, curriculum development, and humanizing policies that can lead to real action and social change! As Dewey (1893) once wrote:

> We have to a considerable extent, given up thinking of this life as merely a preparation for another life. Very largely, however, we think of some parts of this life as merely preparatory to other later stages of it. It is so very largely as to the process of education; and if I were asked to name the most needed of all reforms in the spirit of education, I should say: "Cease conceiving of education as mere preparation for later life, and make it the full meaning of the present life." (pp. 659–660)

We reiterate that what we are endorsing and suggesting here is not just classroom work, but *world* work—that is, planning for and encouraging the type of *knowledge-in-action* that helps students (and those that teach them) to develop and advance the critical dispositions, skills, abilities, and perspectives required to work for equity and justice both now and in the future. It is work that is at once personal, professional, and political. While we are clearly endorsing "big picture" unit plans that span an academic year, this is not the only way to embrace the ideas we present here. Even on a smaller scale, the space exposed at the intersection of critical literacy and curriculum as conversation can provide ample opportunities for transformative pedagogy.

CONFRONTATIONS TO CONSIDER

We are also aware that such classroom and world work will not occur without struggle. As we mentioned in the first chapter, there are currently ongoing political conversations and emerging legislation that represent serious opposition to what we suggest here. Florida's HB 1557, dubbed the "Don't Say Gay" law, has banned public school teachers from introducing texts or engaging in classroom instruction about sexual orientation or gender identity "in a manner that is not age-appropriate or developmentally appropriate for students in accordance with state standards." Likewise, Ohio introduced HB 616 "to . . . enact section 3313.6029 of the Revised Code regarding the promotion and teaching of divisive or inherently racist concepts in public schools" and HB 327 to "enact section 3313.6027 and 4113.35 of the Revised Code to prohibit school districts, community schools, STEM schools, and state agencies from teaching, advocating, or promoting divisive concepts." There is an intentional silencing of voices and ideas across the US.

Alabama, Georgia, Arizona, Louisiana, and others have since initiated serious consideration of legislative ideas that mirror these. What is more, many of these emerging anti-LGBTQ bills have been coupled with proposals that also forbid teaching about systemic racism and the structures of slavery, as well as banning conversations regarding patriarchy and sexism, often on the grounds that discussions about these concepts will create discomfort and promote racial unrest. This type of legislation runs counter to critical literacy and its expressed purposes: to consider the political aspects of literacy education. It also has the potential to make it difficult for teachers to engage in critical literacy pedagogy.

In addition to state laws that use sweeping language to expressly forbid certain types of "classroom talk" and curricular planning, there are documents and plans that appear, on the surface, seemingly harmless if not approached with a critical eye. *Ohio's Plan to Raise Literacy Achievement* (2020), for example, presents a state literacy framework that fails to recognize the significance of the social aspects of learning we highlight here. As literacy educators ourselves, we concede that the document's expressed purpose is to equip children with the skills necessary to be proficient as readers; however, in this case, we would argue that intentionality may not parallel actuality.

This document, rather than considering the socially mediated ways in which children both acquire and utilize their literacy skills, both endorses and encourages a one-size-fits-all approach to teaching and learning reading and writing skills. The state plan outlined in this document negates the impact of cultural values, beliefs, and problem-solving strategies that are inherent in the acquisition of reading, writing, and communication skills. Its utilization of a singular theory—that is, the Simple View of Reading—negates what is embraced by most literacy researchers and teacher educators: that good practice can and should be grounded in multiple frameworks, especially those that embrace the funds of knowledge that students bring to every literacy task and do not privilege the dominant "White" way of knowing, doing, reading, writing, speaking, and thinking. What is more, the document's expressed purpose is to compel schools to align with the state plan.

Educators who teach with an eye toward social justice recognize that literacy events, including reading, writing, speaking, and listening, do not occur in isolation or outside larger contexts. Willinsky (1990/2019) used a bike riding analogy to draw a distinction between literacy as a skill or competence that an individual either possesses or does not possess, and literacy as a greater good, a means for making sense of one's world:

> The point is not to develop the ability to ride, which leads to sessions of practicing and demonstrating the skill . . . [I]f bikes are worth riding then the learning should begin with the intent of taking you places, if only to the end of the block on that first shaky run. What is important about riding are the places to which you ride and the pleasures gained along the way. In the process of this riding with a purpose, the skill naturally improves. (p. 8)

If children are to not only acquire the skills to read but also engage in life-long literate practices, we cannot disengage learning to read from its ultimate purpose. In other words, we are emphasizing yet again that reading should be taught as *knowledge-in-action*—that is, learning for a purpose within a larger disciplinary discourse community. As Muhammad (2020) argues, literacy learning in school classrooms is often grounded solely in cognitive perspectives; this can be seen by a heavy focus on skills-based learning and a heavy reliance on testing data. By failing to take into account the significance of critical and social theories, many schools eliminate the need for a wider range of literacy skills that help children develop critical understandings of themselves, their communities, and their world, and fail to encourage reading and writing skills as a means to shape their identities and align with their purposes.

All education, but especially literacy education, is an opportunity to empower students by embracing the many ways they think, know, and do. As such, we most move beyond the "one size fits all," "one program fixes all" mentality of policy makers and state legislators who create such plans. The idea that there is a prescriptive solution to reading difficulties ignores the fact that "almost all children—including poor children—have impressive language abilities" (Gee, 2007, p. 15) that can, and should, be tapped into through larger language development processes and not just reading instruction designed as "remediation." Our goal, throughout this text, has been to equip educators with a tool kit that embraces not only a wide range of theoretical lenses but also pedagogical methodology that empowers them to make decisions like the professionals they are trained to be. The classroom is the place to demonstrate the relationship between power and literacy, as well as the power *of* literacy itself.

Demonstrating these power relationships can best be done by sharing that power with students. We want to begin sharing power in a variety of ways: by encouraging students to use their own language processes to question their everyday worlds; by helping them interrogate the relationship between language and power; by encouraging them to understand how power relationships are socially constructed and negotiable; and by allowing them to consider personal and collectives actions that move toward social justice. But we want to always remember it is important to prioritize our students' needs, interests, concerns, fears, worries, lived experiences, and background knowledge, not just impose on them a plan for what we believe to be important. That is why, while we endorse the use of the CCCC for long-term educator planning, we recognize that there are myriad ways in which hopeful teachers, who wish to use the ideas presented here, can utilize them in ways that work in their own individual classrooms with their specific students. The CCCC itself can be a flexible, living plan that changes throughout the year.

REVISITING TRANSFORMATIVE
PRACTICES OF HOPEFUL EDUCATORS

Reject Colorblindness

Using the CCCC helps establish a broad, overarching line of inquiry that is designed to value the funds of knowledge each child brings to the classroom conversation. In using the CCCC, educators are empowered to challenge persistent notions that they should avoid the recognition of race (and gender and sexuality). Educators can plan for and engage in ongoing conversations that acknowledge the ways in which race-central experiences shape understandings, attitudes, belief systems, and behavior because the recursive nature of integrated curriculum and critical literacy supports them. Adding critical literacy to this provides a safe space for both teachers and students to question, analyze, resist, and act upon injustice and oppression in a meaningful and powerful way, while still attending to the skills, knowledge, and strategies required by a standards-driven educational system.

Transcend Cultural Conflicts

We have seen that prioritizing one discourse over another is less likely when all participants in a discourse community share equally in that conversation. Sharing power in the direction of the classroom conversation allows all members of the classroom to be active contributors. With the educator guiding from the side, rather than directing from the front, cultural incongruence between teachers and learners is reduced. And we recognize that educators who value and encourage student input position themselves in ways to shed their Eurocentric ideologies. What better way to create potential for promoting justice than to model the ways we can rise above our deeply held biases and preconceived notions?

Confront the Myth of Meritocracy

All members, students and teacher alike, maximize their chance of "success" in the classroom when we value the funds of knowledge of individuals. Teachers can learn to both acknowledge and plan for the many aspects of their students' lived experiences because they engage in regular conversations that help us truly know and appreciate our students and for them to know and appreciate us. Authentic assessments and true engagement become the hallmark of progress and learning, rather than selected response or standardized tests.

Denounce Deficit Mindsets

The "classroom talk" that we have promoted throughout this book affords all students the opportunity to consciously engage, fully participate, and take responsibility for their own learning. BIPOC communities, students in poverty, and students learning English as a second language are welcomed into traditions of learning, using the tools they currently have. Equitable educators adopt a structural view of families experiencing poverty, recognizing that learning outcome disparities result from inequities rather than blaming families for their poverty and students for their perceived lack of skills.

Resist Context-Neutral Mindsets

Teaching and learning must consider the many contexts that surround our teaching and students' learning. Taking a closer look at the systems of power that are at work and confronting and resisting these have the potential to create real momentum for change from the ground up. Organic classroom conversations that explore the many systems in which we and our students live, work, and learn will help us make learning more meaningful and relevant.

CONCLUSION

This big-picture work leads us to somewhere important. Like Muhammad's (2020) four-layered equity framework modeled after nineteenth-century Black literary societies, this work leads us and our students to the following learning goals: (1) identity development, (2) skill development, (3) intellectual development, and (4) "criticality" (p. 12). All of these learning goals can be accomplished in collaboration with students, teachers, and communities—immersed in ongoing critical curricular conversations. Those engaging in useful collaborative critical curricular conversations provide and foster a space for voices that will create change in our struggling democracy. As hooks (2010) reminds us, "Envisioning a future of global peace and justice, we must all realize that collaboration is the practice that will most effectively enable everyone to dialogue together, to create a new language of community and mutual partnership" (p. 41).

We would like to conclude with this caveat. Although we have been tasked with teaching methods for years, we remain suspicious of simple answers and formulaic recipes for what will work and what will not. Even *best practices* and *evidenced-based strategies* are loaded terms that should be regularly, critically analyzed and unpacked. We humbly admit that there is no holy grail, no one answer, for what will work in the classroom because students are complicated and messy—like all of us. We are sure of a few things:

- You care about doing right by your students.
- You believe you can make a difference—and we believe that, too!
- Your hope is foundational to your work for equity and justice.

Becoming a great teacher is a marathon, not a sprint. And during that marathon, the landscape changes, there are unexpected obstacles like path closures and rainstorms, and our bodies and minds fatigue. This is only natural. But it is about living this journey as our authentic selves and reaching out to each other and to our students as grand collaborators for support, love, and care. Because we are all moving in the same direction with similar expectations—to learn, to evolve, to make a positive impact, and to ultimately get to the finish line. The motivation is often intrinsic, built on a desire to do our best and to leave the world a better place than we found it. Our toil is never in vain. We are teacher activists, marinating in hope! Join us.

References

All about Science for Kids. (September 17, 2022). https://easyscienceforkids.com.

Applebee, A. N. (1994). Toward thoughtful curriculum: Fostering discipline-based conversation. *The English Journal, 83*(3), 45–52.

Applebee, A. N. (1996). *Curriculum as conversation.* The University of Chicago Press.

Applebee, A. N. (1997). Rethinking curriculum in the English language arts. *English Journal, 86*(5), 25–31.

Applebee, A. N. (2002). Engaging students in the disciplines of English: What are effective schools doing? *The English Journal, 91*(6), 30–36.

Avi. (2002). *Crispin: The cross of lead.* Hyperion.

Barrett, T. (1999). *Anna of Byzantium.* Dell Laurel-Leaf.

Beech, J. (2020). *White out.* Brill Sense.

Bender-Slack, D. (Ed.). (2019). *Internationalization in the classroom: Going global.* Lexington Books.

Bender-Slack. D. (2020). *The Nicaraguan literacy campaign: The power and politics of literacy.* Lexington Books.

Bender-Slack, D., Miller, A., Imwalle, S., & Stokes, J. (2012). Critical curricular conversations: Merging curriculum theory and critical literacy with pre-service teachers. *Ohio Journal of Teacher Education, 25*(2), 20–28.

Bender-Slack, D., & Miller-Hargis, A. (2014). Envisioning a curriculum of possibility with critical literacy. *Scholar-Practitioner Quarterly, 8*(3), 276–293.

Bergen, L. (2008). *The polar bears' home: A story about global warming.* Simon & Schuster.

Black Eyed Peas. (2003). Where is the love? [CD]. *Elephunk* [CD]. A&M.

Burroughs, R. S. (1999). From the margins to the center: Integrating multicultural literature into the secondary English curriculum. *Journal of Curriculum and Supervision, 14*(2), 136–155.

Camangian. P. R. (2017). *The transformative lives we lead: Making teacher education ours.* Routledge.

Carney, E. (2016). *National Geographic kids: Bears.* National Geographic.

Cherrix, A. (2018). *Backyard bears: Conservation, habitat, changes, and the rise of urban wildlife.* Houghton Mifflin Harcourt.

Cole, J. (2015). *The magic school bus and the climate challenge.* Scholastic.

Cole, J. (Writer). (2017). *The magic school bus: Tales glaciers tell* [animated film]. Scholastic Entertainment.

Collins, P. H. (2009 [2000]). *Black feminist thought: Knowledge, consciousness, and the politics of empowerment.* Routledge. (First published by Hyman in 1990.)

Collins, P. H. (2000). *Black feminist thought: Knowledge, consciousness, and the politics of empowerment.* Routledge.

Crenshaw, K. (1989). *Demarginalizing the intersection of race and sex: A Black feminist critique of antidiscrimination doctrine, feminist theory, and antiracist politics.* University of Chicago Legal Forum.

Davis, D. (Director). (2009). *Clash of the titans* [Motion picture]. MGM Productions.

Dewey, J. (1893). Self-realization as the moral ideal. *The Philosophical Review, 2*(6), 652–664.

Draper, S. (1994). *Tears of a tiger.* Aladdin Paperbacks.

Eisner, E. W. (1985). *The educational imagination: On the design and evaluation of school programs.* Collier Macmillan.

Ellis, D. (2000). *The breadwinner.* Groundwood Books.

Fothergill, A. (Director). (2014). *Bears.* [Film]. Disney Productions.

Freire, P. (1970). *Pedagogy of the oppressed.* Herder & Herder.

Freire, P., & Macedo, D. (1987). *Literacy: Reading the word and the world.* Bergin & Garvey.

Gallas, K., & Smagorinsky, P. (2002). Approaching texts in school: Students understand texts in many ways that may not match the "standard." *Reading Teacher, 56*(1), 54–63.

Gallo, D. (Ed.) (2001). *On the fringe.* Dial Books.

Gee, J. (1990). *Social linguistics and literacies: Ideology in discourses.* Falmer Press.

Gee, J. P. (2007). *Social linguistics and literacies.* (3rd ed.). Routledge.

Giroux, H. (1992). Resisting difference: Cultural studies and the discourse of critical pedagogy. In C. Groosberg & P. Groosberg (Eds.), *Cultural studies* (pp. 199–212). Routledge.

Golding, W. (1954). *The lord of the flies.* The Berkley Publishing Group.

Gorski, P. (2018). *Reaching and teaching students in poverty: Strategies for erasing the opportunity gap.* Teachers College Press.

Gorski, P., & Swalwell, K. (2015). Equity literacy for all. *Educational Leadership, 72*(6), 34–40.

Greene, M. (1995). *Releasing the imagination: Essays on education, the arts, and social change.* John Wiley & Sons.

Gruhl, J. (2020). *Our animal neighbors: Compassion for every furry, slimy, prickly creature on earth.* Bala Kids.

Hall, J. (2007). *A hot planet needs cool kids.* Green Goat Books.

Hancock, J. L. (Director). (2009) *The blind side* [film]. Warner Bros.

hooks, b. (1981). *ain't i a woman: black women and feminism.* 1st ed. South End Press.

hooks, b. (1994). *Teaching to transgress: Education as the practice of freedom.* Routledge.

hooks, b. (2000). *Feminism is for everybody: Passionate politics.* 1st ed. South End Press.

hooks, b. (2010). *Teaching critical thinking.* Routledge.

Hunter, M. (1982). *Mastery teaching.* TIP Publications.

Israel, L. (2017). Wisdom of the heart [acrylic on canvas]. Bears and Bison [original paintings].

Jacobs, H. H. (2004). *Getting results with curriculum mapping.* Association for Curriculum and Development (ASCD).

Joel, B. (1998). We didn't start the fire. *Storm Front* [CD]. Sony. 1989.

Kantor, S. (Ed.). (1998). *One hundred and one African American read aloud stories.* Black Dog & Leventhal.

Kendi, I. (2019). *How to be an antiracist.* One World.

Kilik, J., & Jacobson, N. (Producers), & Ross, G. (Director). (2012). *The hunger games* [Motion Picture]. Lionsgate.

Kress, T., & Lake, R. (2013). *We saved the best for you.* Sense Publisher.

Lankshear, C., & McLaren, P. (Eds.). (1993). *Critical literacy: Politics, praxis, and the postmodern.* State University of New York Press.

Learning for Justice (2021). Social Justice Standards: The learning for justice anti-bias framework. https://www.learningforjustice.org/sites/default/files/2021–11/LFJ -2111-Social-Justice-Standards-Anti-bias-framework-November-2021–11172021 .pdf. Southern Poverty Law Center. Retrieved from: https://www.learningforjustice .org/frameworks/social-justice-standards.

Lewis, C. (2001). *Literary practices as social acts: Power, status, and cultural norms in the classroom.* Erlbaum Associates.

Lewison, M., Leland, C., & Harste, J. (2011). *Creating critical classrooms: K–8 reading and writing with an edge.* Lawrence Erlbaum Associates.

LGH, Bushart, D., & Kaplan, J. S. (1990). The round table: Ghosts of classrooms past? Phase electives, thematic units. *The English Journal, 79*(8), 75–76.

Loewen, N. (2012). *Believe me, Goldilocks rocks!: The story of the three bears as told by Baby Bear.* Picture Window Books.

Lorde, A. (2007). The transformation of silence into action. *Sister outsider.* Crossing Press.

Love, B. (2020). *We want to do more than survive: Abolitionist teaching and the pursuit of educational freedom.* Beacon Press.

Lowry, L. (1993). *The giver.* Dell Laurel-Leaf.

Lyons, S. (2007). *Teens in China.* Compass Point Books.

Mansilla, V., & Jackson, A. (2011). *Educating for global competence: Preparing our youth to engage the world.* The Asia Society.

Mazer, A. (Ed.). (1993). *American street.* Persea Books.

McLaren, P. (2000). *Che Guevara, Paulo Freire, and the pedagogy of revolution.* Rowman & Littlefield Publishers.

Meyer, J., Meyer, F., & Veljkovic, P. (2003). *Teen ink: What matters.* Health Communications, Inc.

Milner VI, R. H. (2010). *Understanding diversity, opportunity gaps, and teaching in today's classrooms: Start where you are, but don't stay there*. Harvard Education Press.

Moore, R., Jensen, M., & Hatch, J. (2003). The problem with state educational standards. *Science Education Review, 2*(3), 1–8.

Morrison, C. D. (2014). From "sage on the stage" to "guide on the side": A good start. *International Journal for the Scholarship of Teaching and Learning, 8*(1), article 4.

Muhammad, G. (2020). *Cultivating genius: An equity framework for culturally and historically responsive literacy*. Scholastic, Inc.

National Geographic Society. (September 17, 2022). https://www.natgeokids.com/.

National Wildlife Foundation. (September 17, 2022). https://rangerrick.org.

Neito, S. (2017). *Language, culture, and teaching: Critical perspectives*. Routledge.

Park, L. (2010). *A long walk to water*. Clarion Books.

Picower, B. (2021). *Reading, writing, and racism: Disrupting whiteness in teacher education and in the classroom*. Beacon Press.

Picower, B., & Kohli, R. (2017). Introduction. In B. Picower & R. Kohli (Eds.), *Confronting racism in teacher education: Counternarratives of critical practice* (pp. 1–17). Routledge.

Powell, D., & Miller-Hargis, A. (2019). Money makes the world go 'round: High school electives that matter. In D. Bender-Slack (Ed.), *Going global: Internationalizing your classroom* (pp. 43–57). Lexington Books.

Ravetch, A. (Director). (2007). *An Arctic tale*. [Film]. National Geographic.

Romano, T. (2000). *Blending genre, altering style*. Boynton/Cook Publishers.

Rosen, M. (2009). *We're going on a bear hunt!* Margaret K. McElderberry Books.

Saad, L. (2020). *Me and white supremacy*. Sourcebooks.

Shaklee, B., & Baily, S. (2012). *Internationalizing teacher education in the United States*. Rowman & Littlefield Publishers.

Shor, I. (1999). What is critical literacy? *The Journal of Pedagogy, Pluralism, and Practice, 1*(4), 1–32.

Sitomer, A. (2008). *The secret story of Sonia Rodriguez*. Hyperion Books for Children.

Smith, D. (2002). *If the world were a village*. Kids Can Press, Ltd.

Stevens, J. (1995). *Tops and bottoms*. Harcourt Books.

Stolley, R., & Sklansky, A. (2000). *Our century in pictures for young people*. Little, Brown and Company.

Tichnor-Wagner, A., Parkhouse, H., Glazier, J., & Cain, J. (2019). *Becoming a globally competent teacher*. Association for Curriculum and Development (ASCD).

Time Life Books. (1993). *China's buried kingdoms*. Time Life Books.

Wilde, K., & Clark, Mr. (2014). The Bear Song. [Single] Self-produced. 2013.

Willinsky, J. (1990 [2019]). *The new literacy: Redefining reading and writing in the schools*. Routledge.

Index

ability, 12, 13, 14, 40, 42, 61, 63
abolitionist teaching, 12, 73–74
access, 9, 11, 12, 39, 45, 85
Applebee, x, xiv, xx, 5–7, 9, 18, 19,
   20–22, 27, 35, 64, 66, 75, 76, 95
Asia Society, 63

BIPOC, 11, 15, 93
Black Literary Societies, 48, 49, 93–94

classroom conversation, 4,
   15–16, 18–23, 27
classroom talk, 5–7, 18–19, 75–76
colonialist, 2, 6, 62, 73
colorblindness, 13, 14, 48
context-neutral, 13, 15, 29, 48, 93
critical social practice, 9, 10, 49, 73, 88
critical stance, 9, 12, 18, 34
culture, xvi, xxii, 6, 9, 10, 12, 14, 15,
   24, 26, 29, 50, 59, 61, 63–66, 68, 70,
   81, 88, 89
curricular structures, 5–7, 21
curriculum: enacted, 17, 19–20, 22;
   hidden, 87–88; integrated, 5–7, 12,
   14–15, 21–22, 28, 33–35, 42, 66,
   78; interdisciplinary, 21; mapping,
   19; null, 88; planned, 17, 19–20, 22;
   received, 17, 19–20, 22

deficit mindset/ideology, xvi, xxi, 11,
   13, 15, 41, 48, 93
dialogue, xi, xxvii, xxix, 24–26, 34, 35,
   60, 64, 94
discussion, 6, 23, 24, 32, 35, 43, 52, 53,
   62, 69, 77, 78, 85, 90
disciplinary discourse, 5, 7, 19, 21, 22,
   27, 33, 45–47, 58, 60, 75, 76, 78,
   82, 84, 91
diversity, 13, 23, 48–51, 59,
   62–63, 66, 73

economic, 11, 59, 65, 69, 70
equity literacy, 11, 15
Eurocentric, 14, 30, 93

Freire, Paulo, 8, 9, 11, 60

gender, 8, 11, 12, 48, 67, 73, 90, 92
global, xix, xx, xxi, 36, 56, 58, 59,
   61–70, 72–74, 94

health, 50, 72, 73
hope, xix, xxii, 4, 7, 8, 9, 13, 16, 41, 60,
   61, 63, 66, 72, 74, 86, 87, 92, 94

identity, 11, 45, 48, 49, 50, 70, 90, 94
IDJA, 48–51. *See also* social
   justice standards

ideology/ideologies, x, 1, 4, 7, 11, 13, 14, 29, 30, 41, 59, 65, 72, 73, 86, 93
inequity, xxi, 11, 12, 88
intercultural competence, 61, 63–65

joy, 49, 74

knowledge-in-action, 9–10, 12, 16, 19, 22, 27, 35, 64, 73–76, 88–89, 91
knowledge-out-of-context, 5, 22, 75

literacy: critical campaigns of, 59, 66; equity in, 11–16, 23, 29–30, 35, 40, 48–49, 69, 73, 78–82
Love, Bettina, 12, 61, 72–74, 85, 86

marginalize, 10, 40, 59
media, ix, 7, 10, 28, 40, 67, 69, 70,
meritocracy, xxii, 13, 14, 41, 42, 48, 93

opportunity gap, xx, 13, 14, 15, 48
oppression/oppressive, 8, 11, 14, 48, 61, 72, 86, 92

poverty, 11, 15, 42, 48, 72, 85, 93
power, x, xi, xviii, xx, xxi, xxii, 1, 2, 4, 8, 9, 11, 12, 14–16, 18, 25, 29, 30, 34, 41, 42, 44, 45, 48, 49, 51–53, 59, 60, 62, 65, 66, 72, 75, 77, 81, 82, 86–89, 91–93

queer leaders, 12
quiet crisis, 47

racism, 12, 67, 85, 90
readability, 6, 39
reflection, 9, 16, 53, 55, 56, 58, 82, 84, 86

resistance, xx, 12, 13, 48, 61, 63
resources, xxi, 9, 11, 20, 30, 33, 38, 39, 46, 49, 65, 69, 71, 73, 80, 83

silence/silencing, 10, 11, 34, 86
social justice standards, 48
social practice: four dimensions of, 10–11
sociopolitical, 11, 26, 28, 47, 59, 81, 82, 85
solidarity, 12, 73
space, ix, x, xi, xx, xxii, 3, 7, 10, 12, 14, 16–19, 21, 27, 28, 35, 49, 50, 64, 65, 74, 77, 81, 88, 89, 92, 94
standardization, 73
standardized tests, xviii, 5, 73
standards, 11, 29, 40, 42–43, 46, 58, 77

taking action, 11, 13, 15, 26, 28, 34, 35, 38, 40, 41, 51, 53, 56–59, 64, 78, 81, 85, 92
traditions: of discourse, 5, 22, 75–76, 78; of knowing and doing, 5, 27, 58, 75–76, 81
transformative courses/pedagogy, xxii, 7, 8, 16, 17, 18, 20, 22, 28, 40, 41, 61, 77, 85, 86, 87, 89, 92

urban, 12, 36, 83
United Nations Sustainability Goals, 72

violence, 71, 73, 85
voice, 2, 10, 11, 27, 34, 35, 52, 59, 62, 88, 89, 90, 94

Whiteness/privilege/supremacy, xviii, 12, 59, 60, 62, 72, 73, 86, 88, 90
whole language, 32